MANX AIRLINES
BRITISH REGIONAL AIRLINES
AIRLINES

Including complete
AIRCRAFT DIRECTORY

Barry Edwards

B & C Publications

Bibliography

Air Pictorial magazine (various issues)
British Airways, Keith Gaskell, Airlife, 1999
Islander News, Quarterly News from BN Historians & BNAPS (various issues), BN Historians
Jet Airliner Production List Volume 2, A B Eastwood & J Roach, TAHS, 1998
Manx Airlines 1982 - 1992, Manx Airlines, 1992
Manx Aviation in War and Peace, Gordon N Kniveton, Manx Experience 1985
Manx Tails, Inflight magazine of Manx Airlines
Manx Transport Review (various issues), MER Society
Modern Civil Aircraft: 11 BAe 146, M J Hardy, Ian Allan, 1991
Propliner Magazine, No36, Autumn 1988
Standard Catalogue of Piper Twin Engine Aircraft, Jim Cavendish, Jones Publishing, 1994
Turbo Prop Airliner Production List 3rd & 4th editions, A B Eastwood & J Roach, TAHS, 1998/2001
UK Airlines, Alan J Wright, Ian Allan, 1998
UK Airports and Airfields (A Spotters Guide), Tim Laming, Airlife, 2000
Wings of Mann, Gordon N Kniveton, Manx Experience 1997
World Airlines Fleet News, No17, November 1988

Copyright 2001, Barry Edwards

Published by
B & C Publications
5 Abbots Close
Ballasalla
Isle of Man
IM9 3EA

Printed in England by
The Amadeus Press

ISBN 0 9527756 4 6

Front Cover

BAe 146/200 G-MIMA (c/n 2079) is based on the Island primarily to operate the London Heathrow and Luton Routes. It is seen here on final approach to runway 26 at Ronaldsway with flight JE882 from Luton on Friday 26 January 2001.

Barry Edwards

Inside Front Cover Top

The very first flight on 1 November 1982 was operated by Embraer E110 'Banderantie' G-RLAY (c/n 110364). The aircraft remained essentially in Genair colours with Manx titling. It is seen here at Ronaldsway in late 1982.

David Ashworth

Inside Front Cover Bottom

In November 1986 a Saab 340 was leased to operate between Liverpool and London Heathrow. G-HOPP (c/n 008) was the first of its type to fly in the UK. It is seen here over the centre of Runcorn from where the crew will have a good view of runway 27 at Liverpool.

Manx Airlines

Title Page

The smallest aircraft used by Manx on scheduled services was this Piper PA31 registered G-CITY (c/n 7852136). It was leased from Island based City Air Links and now operates for Woodgate Aviation (IOM) Ltd. It is seen here at Ronaldsway in the company of F27's G-OMAN and G-IOMA and SD330 G-BGNA.

David Ashworth

Back Cover Top

One of the 21 Short 360's to have seen service with Manx Airlines and British Regional was G-SALU (c/n 3628), on approach to Ronaldsway in December 1989. This aircraft is now in service with the US Air Force as a C-23B Sherpa (c/n 3404)

David Ashworth

Back Cover Middle

ATP G-MANB (c/n 2055) is seen adjacent to the recent extension to the Ronaldsway Terminal Building. The aircraft has completed its days work and is receiving checks in preparation for the following days flying. On a typical day each of the ATP's will fly up to ten sectors. South Barrule can be seen in the distance.

Jon Wornham

Back Cover Bottom

On 24 March 2001 the 18th Embraer 145 G-EMBT (c/n 145404) arrived at Ronaldsway. Resplendent in its British Airways World livery with Chatham Wing Tail, it was captured on film shortly after arriving from Brazil.

Barry Edwards

Introduction

It is now about a year since research into the operating history of the then recently arrived G-MABR prompted a look at the rest of the Manx Airlines and British Regional Airlines fleets. The first list produced contained about 80 aircraft, a figure that has steadily climbed to the 127 listed in this book. The idea of publishing the list was met with the suggestion that an up to date history of the airline should be included.

The history of Manx Airlines and later British Regional Airlines as well is in many ways remarkable, starting out with just four secondhand or leased aircraft in 1982, compared with just over 50 today, the same Managing Director throughout and, from those humble beginnings, becoming the biggest British Airways franchise operator.

The Company was among the first to have the ATP and J41 and was an early user of the 146 jet. More recently it was quick to realise the potential of the regional jet with early orders for the Embraer 145.

Aircraft are listed in the directory by type and alphabetically by the last or latest registration carried while operating for Manx/BRAL.

An aircraft on wet lease comes complete with operating crew, dry lease is the aircraft only with the lessee providing the crew.

A book of this nature calls upon the assistance and knowledge of many other people and I offer my sincere thanks to everyone who has helped. Special thanks are due to Mike Bathgate, Linda Corbett, Ben Cox, Richard Draper, Lisa Duckworth, Alastair Gillespie, Tracey Kinrade, Martin Lampitt, Terry Liddiard, Graeme McFarlane, and Simon Witts all from Manx Airlines. Thanks are also due to David Ashworth, Dave Berry, Tony Breese, Phil lo Bao, Andy Holden, Anna-Marie McLoughlin, John Moon, Chris Sharp and Jon Wornham. The Aviation Hobby Shop, West Drayton and BN Historians have given generous assistance. Martin Nelson assisted with the initial research, my father has once again read the proofs and my wife Carol has as usual allowed the compiling of the book to go ahead unhindered.

Barry Edwards
April 2001

The Embraer 145's have a cruise speed of 451 knots or 520 mph. The early examples delivered to British Regional had both their Brazilian and UK registrations. Here we see G-EMBC/PT-SYU (c/n 145024) in flight during an official photographic session over Brazil. The sleek lines of these aircraft is clearly evident.

Manx Airlines

Manx Airlines & British Regional Airlines

The first passenger carrying flights to Ronaldsway were in 1933, operated by Blackpool and West Coast Air Services. Many names have been and gone since then, including the original Manx Airlines which operated between 1947 and 1955. Fortunes had been mixed and by the early 1980's both Air UK and British Midland were seeing passenger numbers fall sharply. Our story starts in January 1982 when the Isle of Man Airports Board met to discuss these problems and the future of air services to and from the Isle of Man.

At this time services to and from the Island were operated by Air Ecosse, Air UK, Avair, British Midland Airways, Dan-Air, Loganair and Spacegrand who between them served Aberdeen, Belfast, Birmingham, Blackpool, Bristol, Cardiff, Carlisle, Dublin, Dundee, East Midlands, Edinburgh, Glasgow, Leeds/ Bradford, Liverpool, London Gatwick, London Heathrow, Manchester, Newcastle, Prestwick and Teesside.

Passenger figures for 1981 were 292,165 compared with 334,941 in 1980, traffic to Blackpool down by a massive 40%. Discussions with Air UK brought a guarantee that they would not desert the Island but there was no promise that the levels of service could or would be maintained.

British Midland Airways were in a similar position with their Liverpool and Belfast routes, down by 13% and 19% respectively; the only increase was on London Heathrow, up 12%. The overall picture was clear, too many seats for too few passengers.

Michael Bishop (Chairman and Managing Director of British Midland Airways) approached Neil Forster (Chairman of Air UK, a subsidiary of the British and Commonwealth Shipping Group) with a proposal to amalgamate Island routes under one airline. A 50/50 ownership was considered with the London route kept out of the equation but this was not thought to be viable and a 75/25 split

was proposed, to include the London Heathrow route.

Meanwhile, Terry Liddiard (Manager for Handling Services and Route Facilities for British Midland Airways) was preparing a forecast on the future of their Manx routes. He envisaged a low cost Island based airline operating all the current routes and owned by British Midland.

A further Airports Board meeting held in May 1982, this time with Michael Bishop and Terry Liddiard from British Midland and Philip Chapman and Lesley Vondy (Deputy Chairman) from Air UK, discussed and agreed the proposals by the two Airlines, bringing relief to the Island authorities. The formal agreement was signed on 28 July and the start date for the new airline was to be November 1.

Terry Liddiard was appointed Director and General Manager and Captain Norman Brewitt (formerly Viscount training pilot for British Midland Airways at East Midlands) Chief Executive Operations and Chief Pilot. The dormant Manx Airlines name was resurrected, based at Ronaldsway. A subsidiary of British Midland with Air UK holding a 25% stake, the new Manx Airlines was born.

Terry Liddiard took up residence in the Cherry Orchard Hotel at Port Erin, office space was found in Compton House, Castletown and with just ten weeks to go before the first flight, there was plenty to be organised. Employees were sourced from various other airlines; most Island based British Midland cabin crews transferred to Manx with the shortfall

being recruited locally and trained by British Midland.

Uniforms and catering arrangements were soon in place.

The initial schedule was to be three return flights daily to Liverpool, two returns to Belfast, Glasgow, London Heathrow and Manchester and once a day to Blackpool and Dublin. There would also be a twice daily service between Liverpool and Belfast. Fares, to all except Blackpool £53.00 and London Heathrow £101.00, were to be £66.00 return. Liverpool - Belfast was to be £80.00. A 73-seat Vickers Viscount, two 48-seat Fokker F27's and an 18-seat Embraer E110 Banderantie, wet leased from Genair, were secured along with 21 flight crew. Norman Brewitt and local artist Peter Hearsey came up with the livery of light and dark green lines on a white background, apparently having tried every colour from cherry red to chocolate brown.

Route licences were granted, the CAA operator's certificate arrived with just four days to spare, the uniforms with two days but in time for an open house promotion at Ronaldsway on 31 October.

Terry Liddiard had told his colleagues to expect him in the office at the usual time on 1 November, long after the first flight had departed. However, no doubt unable to resist the temptation, he was to be found with his nose pressed against the windows of the first floor viewing area as the Banderantie G-RLAY took off with the 07.35 JE601 to Glasgow. A few minutes later Viscount G-AZNA

At Ronaldsway awaiting its next duty, F27 G-IOMA (c/n 10106) was one of the two used at the very beginning of Manx in 1982. Manx have always taken pride in the appearance of their aircraft and the F27's were clearly no exception.

David Ashworth

Previous Page:
The original Manx fleet included 813 series Viscount G-AZNA (c/n 350) to operate the Isle of Man - London Heathrow route. The large windows of this type afforded the passengers excellent views of the land far below.

Tony Breese Collection

In April 1983 Short 330 G-BGNA (c/n 3029) was leased from Loganair. It began an association with this type and the 360's that was to last into the year 2000 and it is seen here at Ronaldsway in 1983. The most significant difference between the 330 and 360, apart from the size, is that the 330 has a twin tail.

Chris Sharp

Opposite Bottom:
A Shorts 330 was leased in April 1983 and the first 360 in that September. As a result of these trials the Company ordered two new 360's which were delivered in March 1984. The first of these G-LEGS (c/n 3637) is on final approach to Ronaldsway.

Manx Airlines

The Twin Otter operation involved the cabin crew member occupying the right hand seat (First Officer) on the flight deck during take off and landing. Our picture, taken while the aircraft was on approach to Ronaldsway, shows the underwing and wheels to advantage. This particular aircraft now flies for Air Tindi as C-GATU.

Manx Airlines

departed with the first passengers for London Heathrow. F27 G-OMAN arrived from Liverpool at 08.15 and in the evening the Viscount completed the proceedings when it landed from London Heathrow at 20.20. The new Manx Airlines was well and truly airborne.

Following the successful launch and deserved celebrations, thoughts turned to the future and more immediately to 1983 and what enhancements could be made. The Belfast services were re-routed from Belfast International to the re-opened City Airport, reducing journey times by about 15 minutes and for the summer a weekend service to Edinburgh and Sunday only to Jersey via Blackpool were added to the timetable.

During the summer of 1983 a Shorts SD330 G-BGNA was leased in and that September witnessed the arrival of SD360 G-DASI which was leased for daytime work from Air Ecosse. Thus began an association with SD330's and SD360's that was to last into the year 2000.

The one return trip a day to Blackpool with an F27 was proving unviable, due to competition from Spacegrand (later Jersey European) which operated three times daily. A Piper PA31-350 was chartered from Island based City Air Links and took over from the F27, operating four return trips daily, a move which proved so popular that the Piper was itself soon replaced by a DHC6 Twin Otter leased from Loganair. The Twin Otter operation was noteworthy as it was flown with just one pilot, the cabin crew member occupying the right hand seat for take off and landing.

In its first year of operation Manx Airlines carried 235,000 passengers but the accounts showed a deficit of £250,000, some £1million less than British Midland had lost on its Manx routes during 1982.

The two F27's were proving to be unreliable and so at the end of 1983 the leases were not renewed.

Early in 1984 changes outside Manx Airlines were to affect their operations in and out of the Island. Dublin based Avair, which had shared that route with Manx, were forced to pull out. Genair also failed during the year, having operated between the Island and Teesside through the previous summer, a route that they had taken over from Dan-Air who also ceased all operations to and from Ronaldsway at the end of 1984. This left openings to Manx for services to Aberdeen, Birmingham, Bristol, Cardiff, East Midlands, London Gatwick and Teesside if they so wished. A summer Saturday only service was introduced between the Island and Cork.

The trial of the SD360 in the latter part of 1983 had left the management in no doubt that these aircraft were what was needed for services to the Island. The directors were asked to agree the purchase of two brand new SD360's at a cost of £5 million, which they did, the two aircraft arriving in March 1984 registered G-LEGS and G-ISLE.

Passenger numbers on the Liverpool route were still declining and the solution was found in the Viscount which stood idle at Ronaldsway during the day. Liverpool and Ronaldsway airports were persuaded to allow a flight to operate for which they would only charge for the actual number of passengers carried. The 'Farecracker' had arrived, just £18.50 return to Liverpool rising to £20 after the first three months.

The results for the second year of operation showed passenger numbers up to 273,000 and perhaps more importantly a profit of £494,000 was recorded.

1985 was to be as interesting operationally as the two previous years. Firstly, the Isle of Man Steam Packet announced that it was to move its all year round destination away from Liverpool and use Heysham instead. In response to this 'Farecracker' flights were introduced to Liverpool at weekends for the first time, with up to six flights each way each day. Summer Saturday services were added to Birmingham, Leeds/Bradford and Newcastle and Cork was served on both Saturday and Sunday. A third SD360 was introduced to provide the additional capacity. Liverpool passenger numbers for 1985 were 95,000 compared with 28,000 in 1983 and the overall Ronaldsway figure was up to 350,738, the highest since 1979. Manx recorded a profit of £1.75 million for its third year of operation.

A further important development of early 1985 was the agreement with Reed Aviation and the Post Office for Manx to operate a nightly newspaper and postal service from the Island. One of the SD360's was employed, flying five sectors, Isle of Man - Manchester - London Luton - Manchester - Blackpool - Isle of Man.

The London Heathrow route continued to grow and to provide larger and better capacity a Viscount 836 was leased from British Midland Airways. G-BFZL underwent a £100,000 refit at East Midlands and became the flagship of the Manx fleet. 308,000 passengers were carried in 1985

Manx took over British Midland's Liverpool - London Heathrow route at the beginning of 1986, adding a fourth SD360 (G-WACK) to the fleet to operate this service. The 360 was soon replaced by a Saab 340, the first of its type to fly in Great Britain. Later in the year local businessman Albert Gubay

The fourth Short 360 used by Manx was G-WACK (c/n 3611) in early 1986. It later transferred to Loganair and then back to British Regional in 1997. On stand at Ronaldsway it is painted in British Airways express livery. The airport terminal building is in the background and over the front of the aircraft can be seen the original half of Viscount House.

Jon Wornham

In November 1987 Manx took delivery of G-OJET (c/n 1004) a 146/100 series from BAe at Hatfield. It operated the key route between the Island and London Heathrow for around six years before being replaced by G-MIMA in March 1993.

Tony Breese Collection

Opposite Bottom:
British Midland was the launch customer for the BAe ATP, the first example of which made its inaugural flight on 6 August 1986. The second aircraft destined for British Midland was registered G-BMYK (c/n 2003) and first flew on 9 June 1987. Later that month it was displayed at the Paris air show where our picture was taken on 18 June. It was eventually delivered to British Midland on 31 May 1988 and transferred to Manx Airlines in October 1993, becoming G-ERIN in December 1993 and later G-MANL.

David Ashworth

Manx took delivery of their first ATP registered G-UIET (c/n 2006) in October 1988. At Ronaldsway in December 1988, it is in the company of BAe 146/100 G-OJET, displaying both the Manx and Loganair titles.

David Ashworth

made available his Gulfstream Commander 1000 for charter work. July 1986 saw Manx Airlines one millionth passenger arrive at Ronaldsway to be greeted by Terry Liddiard.

As the end of the fourth year of operation approached, Manx had flown over five million miles, carried four million tons of cargo, delivered 23 million newspapers, paid out £5 million in local wages and paid local suppliers and the Airports Board £6 million apiece. Profits for the year rose to £1.9 million with passenger numbers up to 369,000 and so, from a calculated start in late 1982, the basis of the airline had been well and truly established.

The success of the Airline had put the inevitable pressure on office space within Ronaldsway Airport and to alleviate this the Manx Government provided new space on the site adjacent to the terminal building. *Viscount House* as it was to become provided 3000 sq ft of open plan offices and was the first new building to appear at the airport since 1953.

The Liverpool - London Heathrow route was increased to five return flights on weekdays at the beginning of 1987 and a 'Farecracker' service was introduced between Liverpool and Belfast City. The Isle of Man - London Heathrow service was again under pressure for space and so the decision was taken to go for jet operation. The chosen type was the Douglas DC9 and crew training was undertaken but, at the critical point, no aircraft was available. As an announcement had been made that jet aircraft were to be introduced on the route a substitute had to be found. A BAC 1-11 was leased from Airways International Cymru, this type being no stranger to the Island, having been used by Cambrian British Air Services as long ago as 1970 on the same route.

While the re-introduction of the 1-11 was welcomed in some quarters, it certainly was not by the residents of Castletown. It is claimed that on a calm day take off from Ronaldsway could be heard ten miles away in Douglas. Technical difficulties and the limited runway length at Ronaldsway also caused problems.

In 1981 British Aerospace had re-launched a project that had been shelved three years earlier and produced the 146 jet airliner. Soon to become known as the world's quietest jet, the 146 was beginning to win orders from all around the world but BAe had a 146/100 series that they would be willing to lease to Manx on favourable terms. An agreement was reached and the aircraft was prepared by BAe at Hatfield in Hertfordshire. On 30 November 1987, with Captain Norman Brewitt at the controls, it took off from Hatfield, arriving at Ronaldsway just 43 minutes later. The following day 75 staff enjoyed a day trip to Jersey. Three days later G-OJET took off from Ronaldsway with the 07.40 to London Heathrow, slipped quietly over Castletown and made history in London by being the first 146 to land at Heathrow in scheduled service.

Passenger figures for 1987 rose by 21% to 445,000 but profits were down by 28% to £1.36 million attributed to rising fuel costs and higher interest rates.

With the continuing growth in passenger numbers, thought was being given to replacement of the Viscount and in the longer term the SH360's. Various types were considered, the Bombardier Dash 8, Snias Aerospatiale ATR 42/72 and a new product from BAe, the ATP (Advanced Turboprop), for which a party from Manx had been present at the launch ceremony held at Woodford, Manchester on 6 August 1986.

The inaugural Manx flight into London Luton was operated by the Viscount on 17 June 1988, at the same time introducing the 'London Saver' ticket at just £80 return compared with the normal £120 fare to London Heathrow.

In June 1988 the Airlines of Britain Group acquired Air UK's 25% stake in Manx, making the Airline a wholly owned subsidiary of the Group.

British Midland were to be the launch customer for the ATP and the first three aircraft were delivered to them by June 1988. In the July Michael Bishop ordered a further seven aircraft, two for Manx, three for Loganair and two more for British Midland. Two days later British Airways ordered eight with options on a further eight. At over £7 million each the ATP's were expensive and to assist Manx the Isle of Man Bank set up a leasing company, Isle of Man Bank (Leasing) Ltd, to purchase the aircraft and then lease them back to Manx.

In October 1988 a collection party from Manx visited Woodford to accept delivery of the first ATP, which was to bring the Viscount's reign to an end. The second ATP was due in March 1989.

Viscounts had been a familiar sight at Ronaldsway since 1955 when BEA began flying their 701 series to the Island from Manchester. 33 years later on 19 October 1988, Manx, keen not to let this end of an era go unnoticed, organised a series of 'Champagne flights' round the Island before posing

G-BLOA (c/n 259) was an 806 series Viscount used by Manx in 1984 and 1985 on the London Heathrow route, also on the Liverpool 'Farecracker' service.

Tony Breese Collection

Opposite Top:
During 1987 it was announced that the Isle of Man-London Heathrow route was to be upgraded to jet operation. The chosen DC9 was not available and so a BAC1-11 was leased from Airways International Cymru. G-WLAD (c/n 112) is seen here at Heathrow.

The Aviation Hobby Shop

When Manx took over a batch of loss making routes from Loganair in 1994, seven ATP's and three J41's were also transferred. One of the ATP's G-LOGE (c/n 2004) became G-MANJ under Manx ownership. It was involved in a wheel up landing at Liverpool in May 2000 and following the necessary repairs became the first of its type to receive the British Airways World Livery with Chatham Wing tail. It was captured by the camera preparing for departure from Manchester.

The Aviation Hobby Shop

Loganair took delivery of this J31 as G-LOGV (c/n 761) in October 1991 after it had seen service with Alibu Airways. From Loganair it went to Euro Direct and then to Knight Air from where it came to Manx in March 1996. It is seen here in British Airways Express livery. Note that parts of the tail have been replaced and need repainting.

Tony Breese

the aircraft on the tarmac alongside the BAe 146 and ATP. Then as a final farewell the Viscount was to operate that afternoon's round trip to London and what would be the last scheduled operation of the type into Heathrow. The General Manager of Heathrow's Terminal 1 was on the tarmac to meet the aircraft and Air Traffic Control were recorded as saying 'Sad, isn't it?' as they gave the Viscount clearance to take off for its return to Ronaldsway. Just over a week later the Viscount was back at Heathrow standing in for the 146. On 28 October it bid farewell to Ronaldsway and returned to East Midlands.

At the beginning of Autumn 1988 the winter service on the Isle of Man - Dublin and Glasgow routes was improved and the Liverpool - London Heathrow reverted to British Midland.

Passenger numbers for 1988 were 515,000, revenue was £21.5 million and profits up to £1.7 million.

Earlier in 1988 thought had been given to the increasing problem of aircraft maintenance. While all day-to-day work could be carried out at Ronaldsway, aircraft requiring inspections and major work had to go elsewhere. The 146 went to Prestwick, the SF340 to Luton, the SD360's to Glasgow International and the Viscount to East Midlands. Plans were drawn up for a new facility at Ronaldsway that could handle this work. The new £1 million hanger opened in April 1989 and approval was sought from the CAA for Manx to become its own maintenance authority.

The three SD360's underwent a £30,000 per aircraft refurbishment during the 1988/89 winter.

The summer 1989 timetable included a daily service to Birmingham with a day return possible on Wednesdays. A full non-smoking policy on all flights was introduced and the company was nominated for and subsequently won the North West Business and Industry award for the year, Captain Norman Brewitt collecting the cut glass vase at Manchester's Crown Plaza Midland Hotel.

531,000 passengers were carried in 1989 bringing the overall total to over two million in the first seven years of operation. Profits dropped by 24% to £1.3 million largely as a result of higher interest rates and consequently leasing costs, which were up £300,000 to £800,000.

Criticism of high fares, something that does not seem to go away, was countered by comparing full single fares with similar routes of other operators. Isle of Man - London Heathrow was 30.2p per mile, London Heathrow to Jersey 33.9p per mile, Manchester 41.8p per mile and Paris 40.9p per mile.

A third ATP arrived in May 1990, complete with burgundy leather seats and was registered G-PEEL (later G-MANP). The SD360 fleet was reduced to just three aircraft.

The Isle of Man - Birmingham route was increased to two flights daily on weekdays and Isle of Man - London Luton to daily for the summer, leaving only the Newcastle, Leeds/Bradford and Blackpool - Jersey as seasonal weekend services.

A new service was introduced between Liverpool and Dublin with a 'Farecracker' offer, which had proved successful between Liverpool and Belfast. Additionally a new link between Dublin and Jersey, replacing Blackpool - Jersey, was started and a four month evaluation of a Cardiff to Glasgow via Liverpool route begun.

During late summer Manx were approached by British Airways for the lease of an ATP for the winter to operate out of Tegel Airport in Berlin. British Airways already had four ATP's in Germany but required extra capacity. G-PEEL was the aircraft selected and it left on a two month lease, which was later extended to six, on 3 September 1990. The aircraft remained in Manx colours thus making the three legs a familiar sight at airports such as Nuremberg and Brussels.

1990 produced 600,000 passengers and undeterred by profits sadly down again, the airline was looking forward to the new decade.

On Manx routes 1991 was to see the introduction of a summer Isle of Man - Dublin - Cardiff - Jersey service with one return trip each weekday and a jet operated Isle of Man - Jersey via Blackpool on Sundays, the same aircraft also operating a Jersey - Cork return before returning to the Island. However, the biggest expansion was to be away from the Island. The Cardiff evaluation had gone well and so early in the year the company applied to the CAA for licences to operate regular flights from there to Belfast City, Brussels, Dublin, Dusseldorf, Guernsey (Weekends Only), Jersey, Manchester and Paris in addition to the Glasgow route which would operate direct and not via Liverpool. All except Manchester were approved and could start in March. Paris was held back until October when Air France ceased operating the route.

While the operating licences had been granted, to comply with EU regulations the operating company had to be British registered if it was to operate within mainland Britain, so Manx Airlines (Holdings) Ltd was formed as the holding company for Manx Airlines (IOM) Ltd and Manx Airlines (Europe) Ltd, the two new companies being registered on 25 March 1991.

Manchester Airport is the location for this picture of J41 G-MAJA (c/n 41032) displaying the newest Manx Airlines livery. This livery was applied in Spring 2000 when it joined the Island based fleet to operate the daily Dublin and Jersey services.
The Aviation Hobby Shop

In May 1994 Manx took on its second 146/200 primarily to operate the Belfast City - London Heathrow route. It was registered G-MANS (c/n 2088) and in September 1994 went on lease to British Midland and received British Midland logos and titling while retaining the Manx green stripes. It is seen here in this livery at Ronaldsway.
Jon Wornham

Opposite Bottom:
In March 1993 the first J41's were delivered to operate services out of Cardiff. The second of these G-WAWL (c/n 41008) is seen at Cardiff in Manx Airlines livery. It has since been re-registered G-MAJF and currently carries British Airways Express livery.
Manx Airlines

The 54th ATP was delivered to Loganair as G-LOGF (c/n 2054) and became G-MANC in the Manx fleet. On approach to Ronaldsway it displays the older Manx livery to advantage. Later it became the first of the ATP's to receive the new Manx colours.
Tony Breese

An operating hub was set up in Cardiff and two British Aerospace J31's were chosen to operate these services. Fitted out with burgundy leather seats and instead of the possible 19, just 16 seats to allow more comfort on the relatively long flights, G-GLAM and G-WENT began operating from Cardiff on 25 March 1991.

The Ronaldsway hanger facility was now well established and was the world's first complete facility for the ATP's, CAA approval being given for other airlines ATP's to be serviced on the Island.

Perhaps not surprisingly passenger figures for 1991 were up to 625,097, revenue to £31.9 million and profits to £1.61 million.

The expansion away from the Island led the management to look once again at future aircraft. British Aerospace had produced the J41, a twenty-nine seat version of the J31, which was rolled out on 27 March 1991 in the presence of Her Majesty the Queen and the Duke of Edinburgh. At the press conference just two days after the launch of the Cardiff routes Terry Liddiard announced that Manx had ordered two of the type, later increased to five.

Aberdeen was added to the network in April 1992 with a daily service to Belfast City. The Cardiff routes were performing well with the exception of Dusseldorf which was withdrawn, Belfast City and Glasgow benefiting from increased frequency. April was also chosen to launch a new uniform for all front line staff, the predominant colour remaining green.

Tenth birthday time in November was marked by the introduction of a new daily service between Belfast City and London Luton. 'Farecracker' fares were available and soon an ATP was needed to cope with the daily demand. Terry Liddiard attended various receptions to mark the anniversary, including one at Liverpool where in just ten years Manx had become the Airport's biggest carrier.

653,000 passengers had been carried during 1992.

The first J41 arrived in early 1993 registered G-WAWR (later G-MAJD) (Gwawr is Welsh for Dawn) and entered service at Cardiff in February.

While off-Island expansion was high on the agenda, the services to and from the Island were kept under scrutiny. G-OJET had been giving good service on the London Heathrow route for six years and an increase in capacity was sought. The answer was the 146/100's big brother, the 146/200. G-MIMA arrived from British Aerospace in March 1993 and took over the London Heathrow route from G-OJET, which was returned to British Aerospace.

The delivery of further J41's allowed the introduction of two new routes out of London Stansted to Manchester and Waterford and a weekend only Manchester - Waterford in the summer of 1993. The off-Island expansion programme meant that less than half of the overall passenger figures were gained from routes to and from the Isle of Man.

An agreement with British Midland in autumn 1993 allowed the introduction of a new Belfast City - London Heathrow service in November, operated by a second 146 leased from British Aerospace. As part of the agreement Manx bought British Midland's two remaining ATP's and took over their routes from East Midlands to Belfast City and to Guernsey via Birmingham. A tenth route out of Cardiff, to Edinburgh, was also introduced.

The five millionth passenger was carried, among 756,000, in 1993 and projections indicated that one and a half million passengers a year were likely in the near future.

1994 started with the announcement that Manx were to take over a batch of loss-making routes from Loganair (a member of the Airlines of Britain Group). Loganair had begun in 1962 with one aircraft and became part of the British Midland Group in December 1983 when Michael Bishop took a majority shareholding in the company.

Ten years on it was agreed that the transfer to Manx of many of Loganair's routes to destinations outside Scotland would reduce operating costs, as much of the infrastructure was duplicated and could be amalgamated. Loganair's ATP's and J41's were transferred, the changeover taking place on 28 March 1994. Later in July 1994 Loganair became a British Airways franchise operator.

The Loganair takeover came just a few days before an already planned expansion of Manx routes. The combined list of new routes was: Belfast City to East Midlands, Edinburgh and Glasgow; Birmingham to Guernsey; Glasgow to Dublin, Edinburgh and Leeds/Bradford; London Luton to Kerry; Manchester to Belfast City, Brussels, Cork, Guernsey/Jersey, Kerry, Knock, Shannon and Southampton; Southampton to Belfast City, Brussels, Edinburgh, Glasgow, Guernsey and Isle of Man; Stansted to Shannon.

Manx was now operating over seventy

Red Nose day is a well known event to raise money for children in the UK and Africa. Manx Airlines entered into the spirit of the day by applying a red nose to their Island based 146/200 G-MIMA. The aircraft is at Ronaldsway before departing with the afternoon service to London Heathrow.

Richard Draper

Opposite Top:
The first example of the 145 type G-EMBA (c/n 145016) arrived on the Isle of Man on 11 July 1997 displaying both its Brazilian and UK registrations. It left the Island and entered revenue earning service just a week later on 18 July. At Southampton it is being prepared for its next flight.

The Aviation Hobby Shop

One of the 340's leased in during the ownership of Business Air was F-GGBV (c/n 086) from Aigle Azur. It was re-registered G-RUNG by Business Air and now operates for Aurigny Air Services, in whose livery it is at Manchester.

The Aviation Hobby Shop

Loganair took delivery of J41 G-LOGK (c/n 41007) in January 1993. On transfer to Manx it had Manx titling added over the existing Loganair livery. It is seen here at Ronaldsway in this hybrid livery. It was re-registered G-MAJE in September 1994 and now flies in British Airways express livery.

Jon Wornham

routes, with the three legs symbol being seen throughout mainland Britain, Ireland, the Channel Islands and into Europe. Staff had reached 800 and passenger figures for 1994, 1,408,000 but the cost of these major changes caused a loss of £5.1 million to be recorded.

As 1994 came to a close it was announced that Manx Airlines Europe was to become a British Airways franchise partner, joining City Flyer Express, Loganair and Maersk Air. Manx would transfer sixteen aircraft and around 1,200,000 passengers from thirty routes to British Airways colours, with the cabin crews in British Airways uniforms. In return Manx gained the advantage of world-wide sales and inclusion in all British Airways timetables. The franchise agreement came into force on 9 January 1995.

The Manx Airlines summer 1995 timetable was reduced primarily to the Island routes which were to Belfast City, Birmingham, Blackpool, Cardiff, Cork, Dublin, Glasgow, Jersey via Dublin and Cardiff or Blackpool, Liverpool, London Heathrow, London Luton, Manchester, Newcastle and Southampton. Two other routes remained with Manx, Jersey to Cork and London Luton to Kerry. Isle of Man to Belfast City was dropped at the end of the summer.

In May 1995 two ATP's went to Air Ostrava in the Czech Republic on a two year lease, both aircraft being repainted in that airline's livery. The agreement collapsed for financial reasons in January 1996 and the aircraft returned to Ronaldsway.

In November Manx purchased the Island based 146/200 G-MIMA from British Aerospace and in December it went on a three month lease to Air Latvia, based in Riga.

Passenger numbers, including the British Airways franchise routes, fell back a little to 1,343,084 for 1995 but the company once again showed a profit of £1.3 million, although this was against a turnover that exceeded £112 million.

At the beginning of 1996 Manx took over routes from Leeds/Bradford to Aberdeen, Isle of Man and

Southampton, formerly operated by Knight Air which was based at Leeds/Bradford. The Isle of Man - Leeds/Bradford service was re-instated twice daily on weekdays with a single return at weekends. J31's were employed on these services. Isle of Man to Blackpool was dropped at the beginning of the summer timetable.

Emerald Airways, which had for a while been serving the Island for cargo flights, announced in April 1996 that they were to launch a rival passenger service between Liverpool and the Island. This led Manx to introduce a 'Farecracker Extra' service at just £44.00 return compared with the £49.00 'Farecracker'. Passenger numbers for Manx on this route increased by around 20% as a result.

April was to be a busy month. Aberdeen based Business Air was bought and became part of the Airlines of Britain Group under the ownership of Manx Airlines (Holdings) Ltd, complete with seven Saab 340's and a 146/200 which was on lease to Lufthansa. Business Air withdrew from route duplication but continued to operate out of Manchester and Aberdeen and retained its long term night mail contracts.

On 13 August 1996 British Airways announced that it was to withdraw from its six remaining routes to Orkney, Shetland and the Western Isles and that these routes would be operated by Manx Airlines Europe under the franchise agreement from 27 October. ATP's, SH360's and Saab 340's would be used.

On 1 September 1996 Manx Airlines Europe amalgamated with Loganair

and became British Regional Airlines Ltd (BRAL). British Regional Airlines (Holdings) Ltd, formerly Manx Airlines (Holdings) Ltd, still part of the Airlines of Britain Group, became the holding company for Manx Airlines Ltd and BRAL. The Loganair name was retained for trading purposes. One DHC6, five Britten Norman Islanders and seven SD360's joined the Manx/ BRAL fleet.

Passenger numbers for 1996 rose to 1,871,481 of which 574,316 were on the Isle of Man routes. After the losses of 1994 the airline had restored its profits to a healthy margin. Passenger figures for Ronaldsway had climbed from 283,140 in 1982 to 617,653 in 1996 making it the 16th busiest airport in the British Isles.

In early 1997 British Regional Airlines (Holdings) Ltd announced that it was to sever all links with the Airlines of Britain Group and British Midland, enabling it to deepen its ties with British Airways, one of British Midlands biggest competitors.

1997 was also 15th birthday year which made a good start when the Group was awarded the Air Transport World 'Regional Airline of the Year Award'. The presentation ceremony was hosted by British Aerospace at the Castletown Golf Links Hotel on 6 February 1997.

Hot on the heels of the award came the announcement, on 24 February, that the company had broken with tradition and ordered five Brazilian built Embraer ERJ 145 regional jets, the first of which was due for delivery in June with two more due before the end of the year. This order has been increased several times and is

On 24 February 1997 the Group announced that it had ordered five Brazilian built Embraer 145 regional jets to replace J41's on British Airways franchise routes. These aircraft are one of several types that have appeared from various manufacturers in recent years and are becoming increasingly common at UK airports. Offering a fast and comfortable ride, 18 of these are now in service with a further seven on order. G-EMBB (c/n 145021), at Birmingham, is working on lease to British Airways.

The Aviation Hobby Shop

When Manx Airlines Europe and Loganair amalgamated to form British Regional, all the Loganair aircraft became part of British Regional. Among these were five Britten Norman Islanders used for services to the Scottish Islands and the Scottish Air Ambulance service. One of these five G-BJOP (c/n 2132) is about to land at Tingwall during 1998. It is painted in full British Airways World livery and sports the Dove tail.

Loganair/BN Historians

Opposite Bottom:
The success of the Inverness - London Gatwick service which started in 1997 led to the lease of a 146/300 series aircraft from Jersey European towards the end of 1998. In early 2000 the opportunity was taken to purchase one of this type from Ansett in Australia to replace the leased in aircraft. Displaying its Chatham Wing British Airways livery G-OINV (c/n 3171) awaits permission to line up on Runway 08R at Gatwick with flight BA7946 to Inverness.

Barry Edwards

The acquisition of Business Air in April 1996 brought seven Saab 340's into the ownership of Manx Airlines. While under Manx ownership other 340's were leased in, one example being SE-KRN (c/n 159) taxiing onto stand at Ronaldsway.

Tony Breese

currently for 23 aircraft (18 delivered) with options on a further three. These aircraft were to replace J41's on a number of routes allowing an increase in available seats and the shorter journey times offered by jet operation.

Loganair was bought out of British Regional by its management in March 1997, but continues as a British Airways franchise operator. One DHC6 and five Britten Norman Islanders were included in the deal.

The Isle of Man to Leeds/Bradford weekday service was reduced to once daily.

A new service linking Inverness with London Gatwick was launched towards the end of 1997 using a 146/200 aircraft, to replace a recently withdrawn British Airways service between Inverness and London Heathrow.

Business Air, purchased in April 1996, was sold off again on 31 December 1997 along with an increased fleet of 11 Saab 340's, the 146/200 being retained.

Passenger numbers for 1997 topped the two million mark for the first time to stand at 2,232,513 and profits doubled from £1.8 million to £3.9 million. With these results came the announcement that British Regional Airlines (Holdings) Ltd was to be floated on the London Stock Exchange with share dealing expected to start in the summer of 1998.

The delivery of further ERJ 145's allowed Southampton to become an all jet base from February 1998. In the north a number of unprofitable Scottish routes were transferred to Loganair along with the SH360's that operated them. Other Scottish routes out of Glasgow to the Northern and Western Isles were under the punctuality spotlight following the opening of a new line maintenance (minor fault) facility at Glasgow. The London Luton to Kerry service ceased at the end of the winter timetable.

British Airways opened a new terminal (Terminal Three) at Manchester in May 1998 and all BRAL and Manx flights transferred to the new facility.

On 18 May 1998 British Regional Airlines (Holdings) Ltd changed its name to 'British Regional Air Lines Group Limited'. This was followed on 4 June by a further change to 'British Regional Air Lines Group plc' in preparation for the previously announced flotation on the Stock Exchange, which took place on 18 June.

On 9 October the Island based 146 G-MIMA was used to unveil a new Manx Airlines livery which was generally well received and all Island based aircraft have since been repainted.

The Inverness - London Gatwick service completed its first year of operation and in order to increase capacity a 112 seat 146/300 was leased from Jersey European Airways.

The group carried 2,403,153 passengers in 1998 and recorded a profit of £4.6 million allowing it to pay its first dividend of 0.88p per share. Four new ERJ 145's had entered service, with a further six due in 1999.

The arrival of the ERJ 145's meant that the crews needed training to fly them and on 17 December 1998 the Group announced that it was to purchase a 145 simulator, for delivery in May 2000, which would be situated in the Manchester area. This would also allow other UK and European airlines to train their staff in the UK rather than further afield and provide additional income for the BRAL Group.

The penultimate year of the 20th Century dawned with the news that BRAL was to wet lease several ERJ145's to British Airways to allow them to increase some of their services out of Manchester, the first lease starting on 1 February for operation between Manchester and Milan.

A few loss making routes were dropped towards the end of 1998 allowing some new ones to start in 1999. Edinburgh acquired a three times daily service to Paris and from the new Sheffield City Airport services to Belfast City, Dublin and London City were introduced. An ATR 72 was leased from KLM UK to operate between Southampton and Jersey.

The expanding ERJ 145 jet aircraft fleet was putting pressure on maintenance space at Ronaldsway and so a new J41 facility was opened at Glasgow in June to allow the Island to concentrate on the ATP's and 145's.

The increasing age of the turboprop fleet and the ambition to become an all jet operation led to the setting up of a 'Future Aircraft Group' during 1999, to look at the various options that were and would be available. The 'Group' would report back to the Board in 2000.

The announcements about the purchase of two further 146's came close together. A 146/100 was coming from the Debonair fleet to become the 'spare aircraft' and a 146/300 from Ansett in Australia to take over from the leased aircraft on the Inverness - London Gatwick service. Both were due in service early in 2000.

A further six 145's had arrived during 1999 bringing the total to thirteen, while the number on wet lease to

During the early part of 2000 British Regional were offered the 300th aircraft off the Embraer 135/145 production line in Brazil. The aircraft G-EMBP (c/n 145300) flew into Ronaldsway on 27 August 2000 complete with a 300th logo centrally on the fuselage and is on stand 1 just a few minutes after landing. Early in 2001 the author had his first flight in one of this type from Southampton to Ronaldsway, the rostered aircraft, by chance G-EMBP, completing the journey in just 46 minutes.

Barry Edwards

Manx Airlines bid farewell to the Short 360 on 28 April 2000 when G-BLCP (c/n 3632) leased from Aer Arann took off from Ronaldsway with flight JE207 to Dublin. Passengers are boarding the aircraft shortly before departure. British Regional continued to use the type until later in 2000.

Barry Edwards

Opposite Top:
An ATR72 is leased from KLM UK to operate between Jersey and Southampton. G-UKTM was recorded on film, specially for this book, during preparations for departure from Southampton.

Martin McWilliam

On Monday 5 March 2001 Manx resumed flights to Belfast City following the end of Comed Aviation operations. G-MANA operated the Manx service on 12 March and was photographed while on stand at Belfast.

Richard Draper

British Airways had increased to five.

The arrival in early 2000 of the two new 146's meant that in the short term at least two of the 200 series would be spare. In the latter months of 1999 it was announced that they would both be going on dry lease to British Midland Commuter as soon as they could actually be released.

Passenger numbers for 1999 fell slightly from the previous year to 2,359,202 but a healthy profit of £10.9 million was recorded from a revenue of £201.6 million and a dividend of 1.79p was paid for the year.

Cardiff gained jet services to Aberdeen, Brussels and Paris in early 2000. The new 146/100 entered service in February registered G-MABR (Manx Airlines British Regional) and the 146/300 a few months later. It was registered G-OINV, appropriate for the service it was to operate.

British Regional had become the biggest operator of the Embraer 145 outside the USA, and was honoured when Embraer offered them the 300th aircraft to be built, due for delivery in August.

The long association with the SH360's finally came to an end in late June when a leased SH360 left Ronaldsway for Dublin, to be replaced the following week by a J41 newly painted in Manx colours. The arrival of an Island based J41 allowed the introduction of a direct service to Jersey on 3 July. July also saw the refurbishment of G-MIMA incorporating wider but, strangely, fewer seats.

August was a busy month on the aircraft front. Firstly ATP (G-MANJ), involved in a landing incident at Liverpool in May, was returned to the Island. It departed the following day for Eindhoven, where it was repainted in British Airways livery with Chatham Wing tail, becoming the first of its type to carry this livery; the second, G-MANG, was repainted in October.

Later in the month the celebrity Embraer 145 was delivered, arriving at Ronaldsway on a bright sunny Sunday afternoon displaying a 300th logo centrally on its fuselage side which incorporated the BRAL logo in the

second '0' of 300.

Late August also witnessed the opening of a new hanger facility at Manchester, ERJ 145 G-EMBH becoming the first customer on 28th.

During October BRAL announced two new routes, which at the same time opened up two new bases. Work was being sought for the J41's displaced by the ERJ 145's and so the announcement by British Airways franchise operator, Maersk Air, that they were to cease operating between Birmingham and Newcastle, a route that they had recently upgraded from J41 to CRJ 50 jet, was an opportunity not to be missed. At the same time a new service was introduced between Newcastle and Cardiff, both starting on 30 October 2000.

Late October was to see competition arrive on the Isle of Man - Dublin route, with Aer Arann starting a twice daily service from the Dublin end and British European (formerly Jersey European) announcing an increase from three to four flights daily on their Isle of Man - London City route from March 2001.

At a dinner held in London Docklands on 30 November, the Group was awarded the Regional Airline World magazine 'Airline of the Year' award.

Christmas 2000 came twice to the Group, firstly on 18 December when a new engine bay was opened in the former Gubay hanger adjacent to the main hanger at Ronaldsway and then later in the same week, the 17th 145 arrived from Brazil.

The long term objective of the group is

to become an all jet operation, the first step towards this being taken on 31 January 2001 when ATP G-MANU was returned to BAe.

On 20 February, Comed Aviation which had been operating between Blackpool and Belfast via the Isle of Man, ceased operating and so a new Manx Airlines service between the Island and Belfast City was quickly put in place and started on 5 March. Later in the same month two new services started from Manchester, one to Gothenburg and the other to Oslo which had been taken from British Airways Regional.

At the beginning of December 2000 speculation loomed about the possible takeover of the BRAL Group, fuelled by a substantial increase in the share price. The uncertainty about this continued through the first two months of 2001 until at 07.00 on 8 March, British Airways announced that it had made a £78 million bid for the group which the BRAL board would be recommending to its shareholders.

The BRAL Group has become a highly successful operation and was bound to attract the attention of a potential buyer eventually. In the longer term the British Airways plan appears to be to combine BRAL with Brymon Airways, which they already own. Manx routes will continue to operate with aircraft in Manx colours. The only common base is at Manchester but there is no route duplication and so the two can continue to operate pretty much as they are. Brymon operate a fleet of fifteen Bombardier Dash 8's and like BRAL an expanding fleet of (currently seven) Embraer 145's.

British Aircraft Corporation 1-11

Length	107'0", 32.61m		**Wingspan**	93'6", 28.50 m	
Height	24'6", 7.47m		**Wing Area**	1030.5 sq ft, 95.78 sq m	
Cruising Speed	541 mph, 470 knots		**Seats**	97-109	
Range	1700 miles, 2735 km		**Maximum Altitude**	35,000', 10668 m	
Engines	2 x Rolls Royce Spey MK512 Turbofans				

Manx/BRAL Registration	Construction Number	First flew
G-CBIA	166	27/02/1969

Delivered to Autair International Airways as G-AWXJ 20/03/1969; to British Aircraft Corporation 11/1969; re-registered HB-ITK 05/1970; to Nigerian Government as G-AWXJ 19/08/1970 - 10/1970; to British Aircraft Corporation 07/1971; to Robin Loh as 9V-BEF 04/11/1971; to Air Siam 05/1972; to Pelita Air Service as PK-PJC 02/02/1973; to British Island Airways as G-CBIA 28/06/1979; merged to Air UK 01/1980; **to Manx Airlines 10/1987 - 11/1987**; to Okada Air as 5N-AYW 12/10/1989; stored 12/1997.

G-OBWC	230	11/11/1970

Delivered to Sadia, renamed Transbrasil 06/1972, as PP-SDR 31/12/1970; to British Aircraft Corporation as G-BEKA 01/1977; to Arkia as 4X-BAR 08/1977 - 09/1979; to Dan-Air London Ltd as G-BEKA 01/10/1979; to British Air Ferries, renamed British World Airlines 08/04/1993, as G-OBWC 14/02/1993; to Sabena 29/04/1995 - 27/05/1995, 02/07/1995 - 22/07/1995, 27/08/1995 - 13/09/1995, 15/10/1995 - 28/10/1995, 10/11/1995 - 16/12/1995, **to Manx Airlines 16/04/1996 - 29/04/1996 and 21/05/1996 - 01/06/1996**; to Compagnie Air Littoral 08/10/1997 - 25/10/1997; to Air Nostrum 13/12/1997 - 21/12/1997; to Compagnie Air Littoral 22/12/1997 - 04/01/1998; to Air France 29/03/1998 - 06/04/1998; to Debonair Airways 07/04/1998 - 16/05/1998.

G-WLAD	112	12/05/1967

Delivered to British Eagle International Airlines as G-ATPI 25/05/1967; repossessed 11/1968; to Quebecair as CF-QBO 15/04/1969; to Airways International Cymru as G-WLAD 11/1984; to British Midland Airways 05/11/1985 - 05/1987; **to Manx Airlines 15/05/1987 - 10/1987**; to Okada Air as 5N-OVE 08/05/1991; stored 12/1997

British Aerospace ATP (Advanced Turboprop)

Length	85'4", 26.01 m		**Wingspan**	100'6", 30.63 m	
Height	23'5", 7.13 m		**Wing Area**	843 sq ft, 78.32 sq m	
Cruising Speed	305 mph, 268 knots		**Seats**	68 (Manx), 66 (BRAL)	
Range	765 miles, 1,230 km		**Maximum Altitude**	25,000', 7620 m	
Engines	2 x Pratt & Whitney PW126 Turboprops				

Manx/BRAL Registration	Construction Number	First flew
G-BRLY	2025	19/08/1990

Operated for British Airways as G-BRLY 17/04/1991 - 02/10/1991 and 26/03/1992 - 09/06/1992; to Turk Hava Tasimaciligi as TC-THP 27/06/1992 - 25/09/1992; **to Manx Airlines as G-BRLY 26/09/1992 - 31/10/1992**; to British Airways 28/04/1993 - 21/12/1993, 24/08/1994 - 20/11/1994 and 30/11/1994 - 01/07/1995; **to Manx Airlines 01/07/1995; transferred to British Regional Airlines 10/09/1996;** to BAe 03/1999; to Sata Air Acores as CS-TGX 25/03/2000

G-BTTO   2033   29/11/1990

Originally allocated S2-ACZ for Biman Bangladesh Airlines but not used; re-registered G-BTTO by BAe 16/08/1991; to Turk Hava Tasimaciligi as TC-THV 28/02/1992 - 03/09/1993; to Euro Direct Airlines as G-BTTO 19/05/1994, re-registered G-OEDE 28/06/1994; **to Manx Airlines as G-BTTO 14/04/1995 - 12/11/1995**; to Canarias Regional Air as EC-GJU 24/10/1996 - 16/02/1999; to Air Europa Express as EC-HNA 16/05/2000.

G-MANA   2056   23/11/1992   In service in Manx Airlines Livery.

Registered G-LOGH by BAe 31/08/1993; delivered to Loganair as G-MANA 23/03/1994; **transferred to Manx Airlines on the same day; transferred to British Regional Airlines 10/09/1996.**

G-MANB   2055   30/10/1992   In service in Manx Airlines Livery.

Registered G-JATP by BAe 30/03/1993; delivered to Loganair as G-LOGG 27/09/1993; **transferred to Manx Airlines 28/03/1994; re-registered G-MANB 14/09/1994; transferred to British Regional Airlines 10/09/1996.**

G-MANC   2054   08/10/1992   In service in Manx Airlines Livery.

Delivered to Loganair as G-LOGF 21/10/1993; **transferred to Manx Airlines 28/03/1994; re-registered G-MANC 07/11/1994; leased to British Regional Airlines 10/09/1996 - 30/04/1997.**

G-MANE   2045   18/12/1991   In service in British Airways Express livery.

Delivered to Loganair as G-LOGB 27/02/1992; **transferred to Manx Airlines 28/03/1994; re-registered G-MANE 07/06/1994; transferred to British Regional Airlines 10/09/1996.**

G-MANF   2040   14/08/1991   In service in British Airways Express livery.

Delivered to Loganair as G-LOGA 07/11/1991; **transferred to Manx Airlines 28/03/1994; re-registered G-MANF 19/09/1994; transferred to British Regional Airlines 10/09/1996.**

G-MANG   2018   18/09/1989   In service in British Airways World livery with Chatham Wing tail.

Delivered to Loganair as G-OLCD 02/10/1989; re-registered G-LOGD 27/04/1992; **to Manx Airlines 23/10/1992 - 04/1993; transferred to Manx Airlines 28/03/1994; re-registered G-MANG 22/08/1994; transferred to British Regional Airlines 10/09/1996.**

G-MANH   2017   16/08/1989   In service in British Airways World livery with Chatham Wing tail.

Delivered to Loganair as G-OLCC 25/08/1989; re-registered G-LOGC 15/04/1992; **transferred to Manx Airlines 28/03/1994; re-registered G-MANH 16/11/1994; transferred to British Regional Airlines 10/09/1996.**

G-MANJ   2004   17/01/1988   In service in British Airways World livery with Chatham Wing tail.

Delivered to British Midland Airways as G-BMYL 21/03/1989; transferred to Loganair as G-LOGE 25/10/1991; **transferred to Manx Airlines 28/03/1994; re-registered G-MANJ 06/09/1994; transferred to British Regional Airlines 10/09/1996. Involved in wheel up landing incident at Liverpool 16/05/2000**

G-MANL   2003   09/06/1987   In service in British Airways Express livery.

Delivered to British Midland Airways as G-BMYK 31/05/1988; **to Manx Airlines 27/10/1993; re-registered G-ERIN 14/12/1993; re-registered G-MANL 03/10/1994; transferred to British Regional Airlines 10/09/1996.**

G-MANM   2005   11/02/1988   In service in British Airways World livery with Chatham Wing tail.

Originally allocated N375AE Wings West Airlines but not used; registered G-BZWW by BAe 22/01/1988; re-registered G-OATP 20/12/1988; **to Manx Airlines 22/03/1989; re-registered G-MANM 17/10/1994. Nose wheel collapsed on landing at Ronaldsway 23/12/1990.**

G-MANO   2006   20/07/1988   In service in British Airways World livery with Rendevous tail (China)

Originally allocated N376AE Wings West Airlines but not used; **to Manx Airlines as G-UIET 11/10/1988; to British Airways 26/10/1992 - 15/12/1992; re-registered G-MANO 28/11/1994; to Air Ostrava as OK-TFN 17/05/1995 - 09/01/1996.**

G-MANP   2023   01/05/1990   In service in British Airways World livery with Chatham Wing tail.

Delivered to Manx Airlines as G-PEEL l2/05/1990; to British Airways 03/09/1990 - 22/03/1991; to Loganair 27/10/1991 - 06/12/1991; to British Airways 15/12/1992 - 28/04/1993; re-registered G-MANP 28/10/1994; to Air Ostrava as OK-VFO 17/05/1995 - 09/01/1996. Nose wheel collapsed on landing at Speke 19/04/1992.

G-MANU   2008   11/10/1988

Originally allocated N378AE Wings West Airlines but not used; to Ligacoes Aereas Regionais Douro as CS-TGA 25/10/1988 - 21/01/1993; re-registered G-BUUP by BAe on return; **to Manx Airlines 13/07/1993; re-registered G-MANU 20/08/1997;** to BAe 31/01/2001. **Involved in wheel up landing incident at Manchester 04/08/1997.**

G-MAUD   2002   20/02/1987   In service in British Airways World livery with Blue Poole tail (England).

Delivered to British Midland Airways as G-BMYM 17/06/1988; **to Manx Airlines as G-MAUD 31/10/1993 (allocated G-MANK but not used); transferred to British Regional Airlines 10/09/1996; to British Midland Airways 10/09/1996 - 29/03/1997.**

G-OEDJ   2024   21/05/1990

Operated as CS-TGC for Canadian Imperial Bank of Commerce and Ligacoes Aereas Regionais Mondego; re-registered G-BUUR by BAe 21/01/1993; **to Manx Airlines 26/04/1993 - 08/1994;** to Euro Direct Airlines as G-OEDJ l3/10/1994 - 27/02/1995; **to British Regional Airlines 16/08/1997 - 14/01/1998;** to Air Europa Express as EC-GUX 01/06/1998.

British Aerospace Jetstream 31

Length	47'2", 14.37 m	**Wingspan**	52'0", 15.84 m
Height	17'6", 5.37 m	**Wing Area**	270 sq ft, 25.08 sq m
Cruising Speed	300 mph, 261 knots,	**Seats**	16
Range	795 miles, 1280 km	**Maximum Altitude**	25,000', 7620 m
Engines	2 x Garrett TPE331-10 UG Turboprops		

Manx/BRAL Registration	*Construction Number*	*First flew*
G-BSIW	829	05/09/1988

Originally allocated C-FCPG Ontario Express but not used; to Zimex Aviation Ltd as HB-AED 09/12/1988 - 01/06/1990; re-registered G-BS1W by BAe 13/06/1990; **to Manx Airlines 18/10/1991 - 21/06/1993;** to Air Kilroe 07/09/1993; to Euro Direct Airlines 02/09/1994; re-registered G-OEDL 28/09/1994; to BAe 28/02/1995; to Community Express Airlines 28/06/1996 - 10/1996; re-registered C-GMDJ 12/01/1997; to Corporate Express 16/01/1997; to Hellas Wings as SX-BNJ 18/08/1999.

G-GLAM   839   05/10/1988

Registered G-IBLX by BAe 06/10/1988; to Aliblu Airways 18/12/1988 - 17/09/1989; to Air Kilroe 25/11/1989 - 20/03/1990; **to Manx Airlines as G-GLAM 18/03/1991 - 21/03/1993**; to Euro Direct Airlines as G-OEDG 24/06/1994 - 28/02/1995; **to Manx Airlines as G-GLAM 05/02/1996; transferred to British Regional Airlines 10/09/1996**; to BAe 04/1997; to Inglis Aircraft Ltd as ZK-JSA 02/05/1997; to Origin Pacific Airways 02/05/1997.

G-LOGV   761   26/06/1987

Delivered to Aliblu Airways as I-BLUO 09/09/1987 - 05/11/1990; re-registered G-BSZK by BAe 18/12/1990; re-registered G-LOGV 08/07/1991; to Loganair 14/10/1991 - 28/02/1994; to Euro direct as G-OEDA 14/03/1994 - 28/02/1995; to Knight Air 02/1996 - 07/03/1996; **to Manx Airlines as G-LOGV 08/03/1996; transferred to British Regional Airlines 10/09/1996**; to BAe 04/1997; to Inglis Aircraft Ltd as ZK-JSI 24/07/1997; to Origin Pacific Airways 24/07/1997.

G-WENT   838   29/09/1988

Delivered to Aliblu Airways as G-IBLW 15/12/1988 - 13/09/1989; re-registered G-WENT by BAe 15/01/1991; **to Manx Airlines 20/02/1991 - 09/04/1993**; to Euro Direct Airlines as G-OEDD 20/03/1994; to Skyfreighters as OO-EDA 13/07/1994 - 02/1995; to Euro Direct Belgium 01/04/1995 - 15/10/1996; re-registered G-IBLW by BAe 21/01/1997; to Inglis Aircraft Ltd as ZK-JSH 19/05/1997; to Origin Pacific Airways 19/05/1997.

British Aerospace Jetstream 41

Length	63'2", 19.25 m	**Wingspan**	60'5", 18.41 m	
Height	18'10", 5.74 m	**Wing Area**	350 sq ft, 32.59 sq m	
Cruising Speed	335 mph, 292 knots	**Seats**	29	
Range	720 miles, 1,159 km	**Maximum Altitude**	25,000', 7620 m	
Engines	2 x Garrett TPE331-14 GR/HR Turboprops			

Manx/BRAL Registration	Construction Number	First flew	
G-MAJA	41032	30/03/1994	In service in Manx Airlines livery.

Delivered to Manx Airlines as G-MAJA 25/05/1994; leased to British Midland Airways 25/05/1994; transferred to British Regional Airlines 10/09/1996.

G-MAJB	41018	12/07/1993	In service in British Airways World livery with Nolebele tail (South Africa).

Originally allocated N140MA Markair but not used; registered G-BVKT by BAe 23/03/1994; **to Manx Airlines as G-MAJB 10/06/1994; transferred to British Regional Airlines 10/09/1996.**

G-MAJC	41005	20/11/1992	In service in British Airways World livery with Dove tail (Celtic).

Delivered to Loganair as G-LOGJ 08/01/1993; **transferred to Manx Airlines 28/03/1994; re-registered G-MAJC 12/09/1994; transferred to British Regional Airlines 10/09/1996.**

G-MAJD	41006	18/12/1992	In service in British Airways Express livery.

Delivered to Manx Airlines as G-WAWR 03/03/1993; re-registered G-MAJD 27/03/1995; transferred to British Regional Airlines 10/09/1996.

G-MAJE   41007   30/12/1992   In service in British Airways Express livery.

Delivered to Loganair as G-LOGK 27/01/1993; transferred to Manx Airlines 28/03/1994; re-registered G-MAJE 12/09/1994; transferred to British Regional Airlines 10/09/1996.

G-MAJF   41008   09/02/1993   In service in British Airways Express livery.

Delivered to Manx Airlines as G-WAWL 19/03/1993; re-registered G-MAJF 06/02/1995; transferred to British Regional Airlines 10/09/1996.

G-MAJG   41009   02/03/1993   In service in British Airways Express livery.

Delivered to Loganair as G-LOGL 01/04/1993; transferred to Manx Airlines 28/03/1994; re-registered G-MAJG 16/08/1994; transferred to British Regional Airlines 10/09/1996.

G-MAJH   41010   15/03/1993   In service in British Airways Express livery.

Delivered to Manx Airlines as G-WAYR 14/04/1993; re-registered G-MAJH 04/04/1995; transferred to British Regional Airlines 10/09/1996.

G-MAJI   41011   27/03/1993   In service in British Airways Express livery.

Delivered to Manx Airlines as G-WAND 28/04/1993; re-registered G-MAJI 20/03/1995; transferred to British Regional Airlines 10/09/1996.

G-MAJJ   41024   08/10/1993   In service in British Airways Express livery.

Delivered to Manx Airlines as G-WAFT 29/10/1993; re-registered G-MAJJ 27/02/1995; transferred to British Regional Airlines 10/09/1996.

G-MAJK   41070   04/08/1995   In service in British Airways World livery with Wings tail (Denmark)

Delivered to Manx Airlines as G-MAJK 20/09/1995; transferred to British Regional Airlines 10/09/1996.

G-MAJL   41087   23/04/1996   In service in British Airways World livery with Chelsea Rose tail (England)

Delivered to Manx Airlines as G-MAJL 17/05/1996; transferred to British Regional Airlines 10/09/1996.

G-MAJM   41096   01/10/1996   In service in British Airways Express livery.

Delivered to British Regional Airlines as G-MAJM 30/10/1996.

British Aerospace 146/100

Length	85'11", 26.20 m		**Wingspan**	86'5", 26.34 m	
Height	28'3", 8.61 m		**Wing Area**	832 sq ft, 77.35 sq m	
Cruising Speed	460 mph, 400 knots		**Seats**	85 (OJET), 78 (MABR)	
Range	1077 miles, 1733 km		**Maximum Altitude**	30,000', 9144 m	
Engines	4 x Textron Lycoming ALF502 Jets				

Manx/BRAL Registration	Construction Number	First flew	
G-MABR	E1015	16/04/1984	In service in British Airways World livery with Chatham Wing tail.

Delivered to Aspen Airways as N461AP 16/12/1984; to AVIACSA as XA-RST 06/12/1991; repossessed 18/03/1992; Re-registered N568BA 05/1992; to Paukn Air as EC-971 19/09/1995; re-registered EC-GEP 19/12/1995; transferred to Pan Air 03/1997; to Debonair as G-DEBN, **to British Regional Airlines as G-MABR 02/2000.**

G-OJET	E1004	29/08/1982	

Registered G-BIAG then G-OBAF by BAe; to Royal Air Force as ZD695 16/09/1983 - 29/03/1985; to Dan-Air London Ltd as G-BRJS 17/04/1985 - 15/11/1985; re-registered N346SS for British Caribbean Airways but not used; to Dan-Air London Ltd as G-BRJS 22/05/1987 - 07/06/1987; to SATA 27/07/1987 - 30/09/1987; **to Manx Airlines as G-OJET 30/11/1987 - 03/11/1992 and 01/04/1993 - 08/1994;** to Hamburg Airlines 18/09/1994 - 02/12/1994; to Merparti Nusantara Airlines as PK-MTA 09/12/1996; to National Jet Systems as VH-NJA 31/05/1998; to Debonair Airways as G-DEBJ 08/1998.

British Aerospace 146/200

Length	93'8", 28.55 m		**Wingspan**	86'5", 26.34 m	
Height	28'3", 8.61 m		**Wing Area**	832 sq ft, 77.35 sq m	
Cruising Speed	455mph, 395 knots		**Seats**	98 (GNTZ), 95 (MANS), 82 (MIMA)	
Range	1355 miles, 2179 km		**Maximum Altitude**	30,000', 9144 m	
Engines	4 x Textron, Lycoming ALF502 Jets				

Manx/BRAL Registration	Construction Number	First flew	
G-GNTZ	E2036	24/05/1985	In service on lease to British Midland Commuter.

Delivered to Pacific Southwest Airlines as N355PS 08/06/1985; re-registered N175US 11/1987; merged to US Air 09/04/1988; to Crossair as HB-1XB 17/05/1990; **to Business Air 24/08/1993; re-registered G-GNTZ 26/11/1994; to British Regional Airlines 06/11/1997; to British Midland Commuter as G-CLHB 04/2000.**

G-MANS	E2088	21/10/1987	In service on lease to British Midland Commuter.

Delivered to Air UK as G-CHSR 30/03/1988 - 04/09/1992; **to Manx Airlines as G-MANS 05/05/1994; to British Midland Airways 01/09/1994 - 10/1997; transferred to British Regional Airlines 10/1997; to British Midland Commuter as G-CLHC 04/2000.**

G-MIMA	E2079	12/08/1987	In service in Manx Airlines Livery.

Delivered to Air UK as G-CNMF 26/11/1987 - 12/1992; **to Manx Airlines as G-MIMA 13/03/1993; to Air Latvia 28/12/1995 - 17/03/1996.**

In early 2000 advantage was taken of the availability of former Debonair aircraft when a 146/100 G-DEBN (c/n 1015) was purchased as a spare aircraft. It became G-MABR in the Manx/British Regional fleet and is at Ronaldsway shortly after delivery from the paintshop, where it received its British Airways World livery with Chatham Wing tail.

Barry Edwards

The success of the Piper on the Blackpool route led to the introduction of a DHC6 Twin Otter to replace it. Registered G-BEJP (c/n 525) it was leased from Loganair and painted in Manx colours. Here it is undergoing routine checks at Loganair's base in Glasgow.

Tony Breese Collection

The PA31 is the smallest aircraft to have been used on scheduled services by Manx but the smallest to have carried the livery is a PA23 owned by two employees of the company. G-BAED (c/n 273864) is between flights at Ronaldsway.

Jon Wornham

British Aerospace 146/300

Length	101'8", 30.99 m	**Wingspan**	86'5", 26.34 m
Height	28'3", 8.61 m	**Wing Area**	832 sq ft, 77.35 sq m
Cruising Speed	490 mph, 425 knots	**Seats**	112
Range	1253 miles, 2016 km	**Maximum Altitude**	30,000', 9144 m
Engines	4 x Textron Lycoming ALF502 Jets		

Manx/BRAL Registration	Construction Number	First flew	
G-JEAM	E3128	23/04/1989	

Delivered to Thai Airways International as HS-TBK 28/04/1989 - 26/04/1991; re-registered G-BTJT 1992; to Jersey European Airways as G-JEAM 26/05/1993; **to British Regional Airlines 10/1998 - 05/2000.**

Manx/BRAL Registration	Construction Number	First flew	
G-OINV	E3171	09/06/1990	In service in British Airways World livery with Chatham Wing tail.

Delivered to East-West Airlines as VH-EW1 25/08/1990; transferred to Ansett Airlines 27/05/1993; **to British Regional Airlines as G-OINV 05/2000.**

Britten-Norman BN-2B Islander

Length	36'0", 10.97 m	**Wingspan**	49'0", 14.94 m
Height	12'6", 3.81 m	**Wing Area**	325 sq ft, 30.19 sq m
Cruising Speed	150 mph, 130 knots	**Seats**	8
Range	550 miles, 880 km	**Maximum Altitude**	10,000', 3048 m
Engines	2 x Lycoming O540-E4C5		

Manx/BRAL Registration	Construction Number	First flew
G-BJOP	2132	30/03/1982

Delivered to Air UK as G-BJOP 27/04/1982; to Loganair 05/09/1984; **to British Regional Airlines 01/09/1996;** to Loganair 03/1997.

Manx/BRAL Registration	Construction Number	First flew
G-BLDV	2179	26/01/1985

Delivered to Air UK 02/02/1985; to Frisia Luftverkehr, Norddeich as D-INEY 09/04/1986; to Loganair as G-BLDV 12/07/1996; **to British Regional Airlines 01/09/1996;** to Loganair 03/1997.

Manx/BRAL Registration	Construction Number	First flew
G-BLNJ	2189	28/03/1986

Delivered to Air UK 29/04/1986; to Loganair 07/12/1987; **to British Regional Airlines 01/09/1996;** to Loganair 03/1997.

Manx/BRAL Registration	Construction Number	First flew
G-BLNW	2197	28/06/1987

Delivered to Air UK 04/09/1987; to Loganair 23/12/1988; **to British Regional Airlines 01/09/1996;** to Loganair 03/1997.

| G-BPCA | 2198 | 31/08/1987 |

Delivered to Air UK as G-BLNX 28/11/1987; to Loganair as G-BPCA 25/02/1988; **to British Regional Airlines 01/09/1996**; to Loganair 03/1997.

Dehavilland DHC6 Twin Otter

Length	52'0", 15.85 m	**Wingspan**	65'0", 19.81 m
Height	20'0", 6.10 m	**Wing Area**	420 sq ft, 39.02 sq m
Cruising Speed	185 mph, 160 knots	**Seats**	18
Range	600 miles, 965 km	**Maximum Altitude**	10,000', 3048 m
Engines	2 x Pratt & Whitney PT6A-27 Turboprops		

Manx/BRAL Registration	Construction Number	First flew
G-BEJP	525	17/01/1977

Registered G-BEIR by DeHavilland Canada; to Falcon Jet Centre as G-BEJP 28/02/1977; to Baylee Air Charter 04/1997; to Loganair 11/03/1980; to International Red Cross 29/11/1981 - 03/1983; **to Manx Airlines 07/10/1983 - 03/1985**; to Air Tindi as C-GATU 14/05/1994.

| G-BVVK | 666 | 25/01/1980 |

Delivered to Wideroas Flyveselskap as LN-BEZ 14/02/1980; to Loganair as G-BVVK 21/12/1994; **to British Regional Airlines 01/09/1996**; to Loganair 03/1997.

Embraer E110 Bandeirante

Length	49'6", 15.10 m	**Wingspan**	50'3", 15.32 m
Height	16'2", 4.92 m	**Wing Area**	313 sq ft, 29.1 sq m
Cruising Speed	285 mph, 248 Knots	**Seats**	18
Range	1220 m, 1962 km	**Maximum Altitude**	22,500', 6860 m
Engines	2 x Pratt & Whitney PT6A-34 Turboprops		

Manx/BRAL Registration	Construction Number	First flew	
G-BGCS	110207	02/1979	Stood in for G-RLAY on occasions

Registered PT-GLZ by Embraer; then G-BGCR for Ashbon Associates but not used; to Ashbon Associates as G-BGCS 05/05/1979; to Saudia 05/05/1979 - 22/02/1981; to Air Ecosse 03/1981; to Genair 05/1981; to Air Commuter Ltd 06/1982 - 09/1982; to North Canada Air Ltd as C-GPDI 04/1984; to Air Alma 12/1986.

| G-BHYT | 110277 | 06/1980 | Stood in for G-RLAY on occasions |

Registered PT-SBN by Embraer; to CSE Aviation Ltd as G-BHYT 08/1980; to Genair 04/1981; to Skycraft Air Transport as C-GHOY 01/1985.

G-HGGS	110294	09/1980	Stood in for G-RLAY on occasions

Registered PT-SCC by Embraer; to Euroair Transport as G-HGGS 10/10/1980; Crashed into hill near Inverness, Scotland 19/11/1984.

G-RLAY	110364	07/1981	

Registered PT-SEJ by Embraer; to Genair as G-RLAY 11/1981; **to Manx Airlines 01/11/1982 - 1984**; to Euroair Transport as G-BLVG 29/01/1985; to Shachaf Aviation Services 30/09/1985 - 18/11/1987; to Servisair 12/12/1987 - 11/06/1988, and 15/12/1988 - 06/1989; to Business Air 20/03/1991 - 11/1992; to Nyge Aero AB as SE-KES 22/12/1992; to Euroair Transport as G-BLVG 22/03/1994; to BAC Express 19/04/1994; to ATS Air Charter Ltd 06/1994 - 03/03/1995; to Eagle Airways as ZK-DCH 02/10/1995.

G-RVIP	110377	10/1981	Stood in for G-RLAY on occasions

Registered PT-SEU by Embraer; to Genair as G-RVIP 02/1982; to Skycraft Air Transport as C-GHOV 01/1985; to Royale Air Freight Inc as N72RA 04/1994.

Embraer RJ145 EU

Length	98'0", 29.87 m	**Wingspan**	65'9", 20.04 m
Height	22'2", 6.76 m	**Wing Area**	551 sq ft, 51.18 sg m
Cruising Speed	520 mph, 451 knots	**Seats**	49
Range	920 miles, 1480 km	**Maximum Altitude**	37,000', 11277 m
Engines	2 x Rolls Royce/Allison AL3007A Turbofans		

Manx/BRAL Registration	Construction Number	First Flew	
G-EMBA	145016	06/06/1997	In service in BA livery with Dove tail (Ireland).

Registered PT-SYM by Embraer; **to British Regional Airlines as G-EMBA 10/06/1997.**

G-EMBB	145021	07/08/1997	In service in BA livery with Bauhaus tail (Germany).

Registered PT-SYR by Embraer; **to British Regional Airlines as G-EMBB 27/08/1997.**

G-EMBC	145024	20/09/1997	In service in BA livery with Cockerel of Lowicz tail (Poland).

Registered PT-SYU by Embraer; **to British Regional Airlines as G-EMBC 01/10/1997.**

G-EMBD	145039	26/12/1997	In service in BA livery with Animals and Trees tail (Africa).

Delivered to British Regional Airlines as G-EMBD 08/01/1998.

G-EMBE	145042	25/01/1998	In service in BA livery with Waves of the City tail (North America).

Delivered to British Regional Airlines as G-EMBE 03/02/1998.

G-EMBF   145088   14/10/1998   In service in BA livery with Grand Union tail (United Kingdom).

Delivered to British Regional Airlines as G-EMBF 10/11/1998.

G-EMBG   145094   06/11/1998   In service in BA livery with Water Dreaming tail (Australia).

Delivered to British Regional Airlines as G-EMBG 18/11/1998.

G-EMBH   145107   18/01/1999   In service in BA livery with Flower Field tail (Sweden).

Delivered to British Regional Airlines as G-EMBH 21/01/1999.

G-EMBI   145126   15/04/1999   In service in BA livery with Paithani tail (India).

Delivered to British Regional Airlines as G-EMBI 23/04/1999.

G-EMBJ   145134   06/05/1999   In service in BA livery with Youm al-Suq tail (Saudi Arabia).

Delivered to British Regional Airlines as G-EMBJ 24/05/1999.

G-EMBK   145167   13/08/1999   In service in BA livery with Benyhone tail (Scotland).

Delivered to British Regional Airlines as G-EMBK 26/08/1999.

G-EMBL   145177   13/09/1999   In service in BA livery with Chatham Wing tail (United Kingdom).

Delivered to British Regional Airlines as G-EMBL 04/10/1999.

G-EMBM   145196   11/11/1999   In service in BA livery with Chatham Wing tail (United Kingdom).

Delivered to British Regional Airlines as G-EMBM 22/11/1999.

G-EMBN   145201   02/12/1999   In service in BA livery with Chatham Wing tail (United Kingdom).

Delivered to British Regional Airlines as G-EMBN 13/01/2000.

G-EMBO   145219   11/01/2000   In service in BA livery with Chatham Wing tail (United Kingdom).

Delivered to British Regional Airlines as G-EMBO 14/03/2000.

G-EMBP   145300   26/07/2000   In service in BA livery with Chatham Wing tail (United Kingdom).

Registered PT-SKR by Embraer; to British Regional Airlines as G-EMBP 25/08/2000.

G-EMBS   145357   12/12/2000   In service in BA livery with Chatham Wing tail (United Kingdom).

Delivered to British Regional Airlines as G-EMBS 20/12/2000

G-EMBT   145404   16/03/2001   In service in BA livery with Chatham Wing tail (United Kingdom).

Delivered to British Regional Airlines as G-EMBT 21/03/2001

G-EMBU	145458	On order for delivery June 2001
G-EMBV	145	On order for delivery August 2001
G-EMBW	145	On order for delivery December 2001
G-EMBX	145	On order for delivery March 2002
G-EMBY	145	On order for delivery July 2002
G-EMBZ	145	On order for delivery September 2002

Fokker F27

Length	82'2", 25.06 m	**Wingspan**	95'2", 29.0 m
Height	28'7", 8.71 m	**Wing Area**	753.5 sq ft, 70.0 sq m
Cruising Speed	300 mph, 259 Knots	**Seats**	48
Range	1080 miles, 1741Km	**Maximum Altitude**	29,500', 8990 m
Engines	2x Rolls Royce Dart Mk552 Turboprops		

Manx/BRAL Registration	Construction Number	First flew
G-IOMA	10106	16/06/1958

Registered PH-FAB by Fokker; to Aer Lingus as EI-AKB 19/11/1958; to Philippine Airlines as PI-C530 17/01/1966; to Fokker as PH-FSH 24/04/1967; to Alia Royal Jordanian Airlines as JY-ADD 26/04/1967 - 25/09/1967; to Spantax SA as EC-BNJ 09/11/1967; to Aviaco 01/04/1976; to Air Classic as D-BOBY 08/1981; to WDL Flugdienst 11/1981; **to Manx Airlines as G-IOMA 21/09/1982 - 27/09/1983**; to Loganair 20/11/1983; to Short Brothers 04/1986; to Tal Air 05/1986; to Fortis Aviation Inc as G-BMZI 21/10/1986; to WDL Flugdienst 21/10/1986; to WDL Flugdienst as D-BAKO 05/1987; to FTG Air Service Flug-charter 05/1990; to Field Aviation 02/1991; merged with WDL Flugdienst 01/10/1991; to Aircraft Financing & Trading BV 30/10/1995; to Swetrail AB 13/04/1996; to fire practice at Vasteras, Sweden 04/1996.

G-OMAN	10120	21/05/1959

Registered PH-FAP by Fokker; to Trans Australia Airlines as VH-TFE 06/06/1959; to Australian Department of Aviation 25/03/1966; to Air Anglia 28/07/1978; re-registered G-SPUD 31/01/1979; merged Air UK 16/01/1980; to Nile Delta Air Services 19/08/1981 - 09/1982; **to Manx Airlines as G-OMAN 10/1982 - 04/03/1984**; stored Norwich, Norfolk as G-BLFJ 11/1994; Broken up 12/1996.

The other F27 was G-OMAN (c/n 10120) seen here moving off stand 4 at Ronaldsway. The cabin crew will be about to go through the all important safety briefing for the passengers while the Captain and First Officer will be ensuring that they have the correct clearance and checking the weather at their destination.

Tony Breese Collection

Gulfstream Commander 1000

Length	43'0", 13.10 m	**Wingspan**	52'1", 15.89 m	
Height	14'11", 4.56 m	**Wing Area**	279.3 sq ft, 25.95 sq m	
Cruising Speed		**Seats**	6-7	
Range		**Maximum Altitude**		
Engines	2 x Garrett TPE331-10-501K Turboprops			

Manx/BRAL Registration	Construction Number	First flew	
G-YABU	96083		Chartered from Mr A Gubay

Piper PA23-250 Aztec

Length	30'2", 9.19 m	**Wingspan**	37'2", 11.33 m	
Height	10'3", 3.12 m	**Wing Area**	207.6 sq ft, 19.3 sq m	
Cruising Speed	210 mph, 182 knots	**Seats**	5	
Range	1100 m, 1770 km	**Maximum Altitude**	21,000', 6400 m	
Engines	2 x Lycoming IO 540-C45B			

Manx/BRAL Registration	Construction Number	First flew	
G-BAED	27-3864	c1958	In old Manx Airlines Livery but not part of the official fleet.

Owned by N Brewitt & K Manktelow. Sold and transferred to the USA register 01/2000

Piper PA31-350 Navajo Chieftan

Length	37'7", 11.45 m	**Wingspan**	40'8", 12.4 m	
Height	13'0", 3.96 m	**Wing Area**	229.0 sq ft, 21.28 sq m	
Cruising Speed	250 mph, 217 knots	**Seats**	10	
Range	1100 miles, 1770 km	**Maximum Altitude**	24,000', 7315 m	
Engines	2 x Lycoming T10-540-J2BD			

Manx/BRAL Registration	Construction Number	First flew
G-CITY	31-7852136	1978

Registered N27741 by Piper Aircraft; delivered to City Air Links as G-CITY 1978; **to Manx Airlines 05/1983 - 07/10/1983**; to Woodgate Aviation (IOM) Ltd

Saab SF340

Length	64'8", 19.71 m	
Height	22'6", 6.86 m	
Cruising Speed	285 mph, 250 knots	
Range	809 miles, 1300 km	
Engines	2 x GE CT75A2 Turboprops	

Wingspan	70'4", 21.43 m	
Wing Area	450 sq ft, 41.81 sq m	
Seats	34	
Maximum Altitude	25,000', 7620 m	

Manx/BRAL Registration	*Construction Number*	*First flew*
G-GNTA	049	27/02/1986

Delivered to Crossair as HB-AHH 19/03/1986; **to Business Air as G-GNTA 30/03/1991**; to Air Rarotonga as ZK-EFS 06/2000.

G-GNTB	082	28/01/1987

Delivered to Crossair as HB-AHL 06/03/1987; **to Business Air 13/09/1990; to British Airways 29/10/1990 - 28/03/1991; re-registered G-GNTB 30/09/1991;** to Saab 07/06/2000; to Aurigny Air Services 09/06/2000.

G-GNTC	020	21/04/1985

Delivered to Crossair as HB-AHE 27/03/1985; to Tatra Air as OK-RGS 28/03/1991 - 01/04/1992; **to Business Air as HB-AHE 12/07/1992; re-registered G-GNTC 26/09/1992;** to Saab 07/1999; to Aurigny Air Services 30/09/1999.

G-GNTD	100	08/08/1987

Delivered to Salair as SE-ISK 04/09/1987; merged Avia 01/08/1991 and renamed Skyways 01/09/1992; **to Business Air as G-GNTD 31/12/1992;** to British Midland Commuter 2000.

G-GNTE	133	11/10/1988	In service in British Airways World livery with Benyhone tail (Scotland)

Delivered to Salair as SE-ISM 11/11/1988; merged Avia 01/08/1991 and renamed Skyways 01/09/1992; **to Business Air 04/01/1993; re-registered G-GNTE 22/01/1993; to British Regional Airlines 01/01/1998.**

G-GNTF	113	13/01/1988

Delivered to Crossair as HB-AHO 19/02/1988; **to Business Air as G-GNTF 27/10/1994;** to British Midland Commuter 2000.

G-GNTG	126	28/06/1988

Delivered to Crossair as HB-AHR 08/1988; to Swedair 29/05/1990 - 26/06/1990; **to Business Air 01/10/1994; re-registered G-GNTG 18/11/1994;** to British Midland Commuter 2000.

G-GNTH	169	27/10/1989

Delivered to Metroflight as N588MA 15/12/1989; merged Simmons Airlines 28/05/1993; **to Business Air as G-GNTH 17/01/1997;** to British Midland Commuter 2000.

G-GNTI	172	25/11/1989

Delivered to Metroflight as N589MA 21/12/1989; merged Simmons Airlines 28/05/1993; **to Business Air as G-GNTI 20/12/1996; to British Midland Airways 03/1997;** to British Midland Commuter 2000.

G-GNTJ   192   24/04/1990

Delivered to Metroflight as N591MA 09/06/1990; merged Simmons Airlines 28/05/1993; **to Business Air as G-GNTJ 26/02/1997**; to British Midland Commuter 2000.

G-HOPP   008   04/08/1984

Delivered to Birmingham Executive Airways as G-BSFI 27/12/1984; to Saab as SE-ISC 13/12/1985; to Swedair 19/08/1986 - 10/1986; **to Manx Airlines as G-HOPP 29/11/1986 - 26/10/1988**; to VAG Sverige AB as SE-ISC 01/11/1988; to Brittany Air International 03/11/1988 - 12/1988; to Netherlines as PH-KJK 17/02/1989; merged KLM Cityhopper 01/08/1990; to Kendell Airlines as VH-KDB 26/11/1991.

G-RUNG   086   03/03/1987

Delivered to Air Limousin as F-GGBV 25/03/1987 - 31/01/1990; to Aigle Azur 01/02/1990; to Business Air 17/07/1994 - 30/09/1994; to Regional Airlines 03/1995 - 09/1995; **to Business Air 06/05/1996 - 10/06/1996 and 01/05/1997; re-registered G-RUNG 03/06/1997**; to Aurigny Air Services 23/06/1999.

SE-KFA   132   08/10/1988

Delivered to Crossair as HB-AHS 09/11/1988; to Prima Air as EC-229 22/02/1996; re-registered EC-GGK 07/1996; **to Business Air as SE-KFA 05/11/1996 - 19/03/1997**; to Air Ostrava as OK-TOP 06/04/1997; to Slovak Airlines 01/01/1998 - 06/1998 and as OM-BAA 07/1999 - 11/02/2000; to Saab 01/03/2000; re-registered SE-LMT 05/2000; to Max Air 2000.

SE-KRN   159   17/08/1989

Originally allocated SE-ISI Salair but not used; to Salenia Aviation AB as D-CHBC 17/10/1989; to Air Bremen 17/10/1989; to Salenia Aviation AB 22/08/1990; to VAG Sverige AB as SE-KRN 05/01/1991; to Salair 05/01/1991; merged Avia 01/08/1991 and renamed Skyways 01/09/1992; to Air Baltic 01/10/1995 - 10/11/1995; **to Business Air 10/1996 - 23/12/1996.**

Short Brothers SD330

Length	58'0", 17.69 m		**Wingspan**	74'8", 22.76 m
Height	16'3", 4.95 m		**Wing Area**	453 sq ft, 42.1 sq m
Cruising Speed	218 mph, 190 knots		**Seats**	30
Range	1053 miles, 1695 km		**Maximum Altitude**	11,500', 3500 m
Engines	C/n 3001-26	2x Pratt & Whitney PT6A 45A Turboprops		
	C/n 3027-67	2x Pratt & Whitney PT6A 45B Turboprops		
	C/n 3068 onwards	2x Pratt & Whitney PT6A 45R Turboprops		

Manx/BRAL Registration	Construction Number	First flew
G-BGNA	SH3029	31/05/1979

Delivered to Loganair as G-BGNA 28/06/1979; **to Manx Airlines 17/04/1983**; to Air Ecosse 01/11/1983; to Short Brothers 03/1984; to Metropolitan Airways 24/03/1984 - 02/09/1985; re-registered G-BTJR 30/11/1985; to Syd-Aero, renamed Avia 01/01/1988, as SE-IVX 24/09/1986; to Queensland Pacific Airlines as VH-LSI 09/12/1989; to Sunstate Airlines 25/10/1990; to Chartair 19/02/1996; transferred to Airnorth Central 02/1996; to Corporate Air as N334AC 20/04/1998; to Air Cargo Carriers 11/1998.

G-BIOF   SH3064   20/02/1981

Registered G-BIOF then N4270A by Short Brothers; to Coral Air 23/03/1981; re-registered N28OVY 05/1981; to Short Brothers 04/1982; to Pennsylvania Airlines 06/1982 - 12/1982; to Command Airways 12/1982 - 03/1983; to Fischer Brothers Aviation 12/04/1983 - 06/1983; to Avair as EI-BNM 06/1983; repossessed 24/02/1984; to Air Ecosse as G-BIOF 05/1984; to Air UK 05/1984; **to Manx Airlines 07/1984 - 08/1984;** to Okada Air as 5N-AOX 13/09/1985; to Short Brothers 31/06/1986; to Janes Aviation as G-LEDN 20/01/1989; to Short Brothers 12/1991; to Titan Airways 12/1991; to Streamline Aviation 25/03/1993; re-registered G-SSWN 03/03/2000; damaged beyond repair at Paris Charles de Gaulle 25/05/2000.

G-BKMU   SH3092   24/03/1983

Registered G-BKMU by Short Brothers; to Aer Lingus Commuter as EI-BEG 11/04/1983; re-registered EI-BEH 25/05/1983; to Short Brothers as G-BKMU 29/11/1984; to Fairflight Charters Ltd 02/1985; **to Manx Airlines 04/03/1985 - 07/1985;** to Guernsey Airlines 08/1985 - 13/07/1987; to Short Brothers 21/07/1987; to Syd-Aero, renamed Avia AB, as SE-IYO 29/08/1987 - 11/1990; to Titan Airways as G-BKMU 01/04/1992 - 07/1992; to EI Air Exports as EI-EXP 13/08/1992; to Ireland Airways 08/1995; to Emerald Airways 01/09/1995 - 09/1996; to Ireland Airways 10/1997; stored Exeter, Devon 02/1998; broken up 02/1999.

Shorts Brothers SD360

Length	70'10", 21.59 m	**Wingspan**	74'10", 22.80 m	
Height	23'8", 7.21 m	**Wing Area**	454 sq ft, 42.18 sq m	
Cruising Speed	244 mph, 210 knots	**Seats**	36	
Range	1055 miles, 1697 km	**Maximum Altitude**	10,000', 3048 m	
Engines	2 x Pratt & Whitney PT6A-65R Turboprops			

Manx/BRAL Registration	Construction Number	First flew	
EI-CPR	SH3713	03/02/1987	Used on IOM - Dublin, wet leased from Aer Arann.

Registered G-BNDJ by Short Brothers but not used; to Jersey European Airways as G-OBOH 03/03/1987; to Community Express Airlines 24/05/1996 - 17/10/1996; to BAC Express 31/10/1996; to Aer Arann 28/04/1998 - 11/1998 and as EI-CPR 21/01/1999.

G-BKMX   SH3608   11/03/1983

Delivered to Loganair as G-BKMX 22/03/1983; **to Manx Airlines 06/1988 - 20/02/1994; transferred to British Regional Airlines 24/01/1997;** to Jersey European Airways 15/10/1998; to BAC Express 06/2000.

G-BLCP   SH3632   06/01/1984   Used on IOM - Dublin, wet leased from Aer Arann.

Delivered to Air Business, renamed Maersk Commuter 01/06/1988, as OY-MMA 12/01/1984; to Aer Lingus Commuter as EI-BYU 13/10/1989 - 29/10/1990; transferred to Maersk Air as OY-MMA 24/03/1992; to Muk Air Taxi 29/06/1993; to BAC Express as G-BLCP 07/06/1999; to Aer Arann 21/06/1999 - 18/05/2000; to Aerocondor Transportes Aereos 12/07/2000.

G-BLGB   SH3641   27/03/1984

Delivered to Loganair as G-BLGB 30/03/1984; **transferred to British Regional Airlines 27/01/1997; Involved in Wheels up Landing incident at Stornoway and withdrawn from use 09/02/1998.**

The 86th Short 360 was delivered to British Midland as G-BMHX (c/n 3686) in May 1986. It saw service with Manx in 1987 before joining the Loganair fleet. It is in Loganair livery that it is seen here at Ronaldsway. This aircraft has recently gone to Streamline Aviation as G-SSWC.

Tony Breese Collection

One of the early Short 360's operated by Manx was G-DASI (c/n 3606). It came from Air Ecosse and eventually saw service with Gill Airways in whose livery it is seen here at Ronaldsway. It was broken up in October 2000.

Jon Wornham

Manx Airlines opened its new hanger facility at Ronaldsway in March 1989. Here we see ATP G-MANM (c/n 2005) undergoing a full inspection inside the hanger.

Manx Airlines

G-BMAR   SH3633   20/01/1984

Delivered to British Midland Airways as G-BMAR 23/03/1984; **to Manx Airlines 22/05/1986**; to Loganair 03/10/1986; to British Midland Airways 19/05/1994; to Cityflyer Express 01/06/1994 - 11/1994; to Loganair 03/1995; **transferred to British Regional Airlines 27/01/1997**; to BAC Express 18/12/1998; to Pacific Coastal Airlines as C-GPCT 05/1999.

G-BMHX   SH3686   14/01/1986

Delivered to British Midland Airways as G-BMHX 02/05/1986; **to Manx Airlines 05/1987 - 06/1987**; to Loganair 08/11/1988; to Short Brothers 12/10/1995; to Flying Enterprise as SE-LGE 06/08/1996; to Streamline Aviation (SW) Ltd as G-SSWC 11/2000.

G-BMHY   SH3687   21/01/1986   Known to have been used but no details available

Delivered to British Midland Airways as G-BMHY 21/05/1986; to Short Brothers 13/09/1988; to Aer Lingus Commuter 07/03/1989 - 10/04/1989; to Guernsey Airlines 04/1989; merged to Air Europe Express 1989, to 15/03/1991; to Euroworld Airways, renamed Cityflyer Express 03/02/1992, as G-OREX 30/05/1991 - 01/11/1993; re-registered N428SA 01/1995; Converted to C-23B Sherpa (c/n 3414) 09/1997; to United States Air Force as 93-1322 10/1997.

G-BMLC   SH3688   05/02/1986   Known to have been used but no details available

Delivered to British Midland Airways as G-BMLC 25/04/1986; to Loganair 25/04/1986; to Flying Enterprise as SE-LDA 02/04/1996; to Aurigny Air Services as G-BMLC 24/05/2000.

G-BVMY   SH3755   31/03/1989

Registered G-BPKY then G-OEEC by Short Brothers; to Capital Airlines 27/04/1989; repossessed 08/10/1990; to Cityflyer Express as G-BVMY 26/11/1993 - 29/10/1995; **to Loganair 21/11/1995; transferred to British Regional Airlines 27/01/1997**; to Shorts Brothers 11/1997; to Flying Enterprise as SE-LHY 25/11/1997.

G-CEAL   SH3761   03/11/1989   Used on Belfast - Edinburgh leased from BAC Express.

Registered G-BPX0 then N161SB by Short Brothers; to Crown Airways, renamed Liberty Express 06/1993,01/1990; re-registered N161CN 04/1991; to Community Express Airlines as G-CEAL 11/09/1995 - 09/1996; to BAC Express Airlines 10/01/1997.

G-CLAS   SH3635   01/02/1984

Delivered to Aer Lingus Commuter as EI-BEK 08/03/1984; to Caledonian Airborne Systems Ltd as G-CLAS 21/07/1993; to Bon-Accord Airways 21/07/1993; to BAC Express 21/11/1995; **to Manx Airlines 01/1997 - 2000.**

G-DASI   SH3606   16/02/1983

Delivered to Air Ecosse as G-DASI 22/02/1983; **to Manx Airlines 09/1983 - 04/1984**; to Air Business 10/08/1984 - 07/09/1984; to Air UK 12/09/1984; to Gill Air, renamed Gill Airways 24/06/1995, 01/04/1995; broken up 10/2000.

G-EXPS   SH3661   07/01/1985   Used on Belfast - Edinburgh leased from BAC Express.

Delivered to Fairflight Charters Ltd as G-BLRT 12/01/1985; to Air Ecosse 12/01/1985; to Air Business 08/04/1985 - 28/06/1985 and 22/09/1985 - 09/1985; to Air Lingus Commuter 02/11/1986 - 01/12/1986; to Fairfight Charters Ltd 07/12/1986; to Air UK 24/08/1987 - 12/1987; to Guernsey Airlines 29/12/1987; to Short Brothers 07/09/1988; to Guernsey Airlines 07/09/1988; merged Air Europe Express 29/10/1989; to Short Brothers 29/10/1990; to Avia AB as SE-KRV 30/11/1990; to LFG Aviation Ltd 03/10/1991; to Air Hudik 04/10/1991; to Shorts brothers as G-BLRT 01/04/1992; to Sonmez Airlines 26/05/1993; re-registered TC-AOA 16/06/1993; to BAC Express as G-EXPS 05/1999; to Aurigny Air Services 25/04/2000 - 2000.

G-ISLE   SH3638   01/03/1984

Delivered to Manx Airlines as G-ISLE 28/03/1984; to Loganair 12/1994; transferred to British Regional Airlines 23/01/1997; to ATA Aerocondor as CS-TMN 01/1999.

G-KBAC   SH3758   16/08/1989   Used on Belfast - Edinburgh wet leased from BAC Express.

Registered G-BPXL by Short Brothers; to Hazelton Airlines as VH-MJH 01/09/1989; to BAC Express as G-KBAC 15/12/1997; to Gill Airways 26/01/1998 - 04/02/2000.

G-LEGS   SH3637   23/02/1984

Delivered to Manx Airlines as G-LEGS 09/03/1984; to Loganair 12/1994; transferred to British Regional Airlines 23/01/1997; to Loganair 11/1998; to BAC Express 08/01/1999; to Associated Aviation Ltd as 5N-BBL 17/03/2000.

G-OJSY   SH3603   10/12/1982   Known to have been used but no details available

Registered G-BKKT by Short Brothers 12/1982; to Genair 20/12/1982; repossessed 24/10/1984; to Simmons Airlines as N368MQ 10/1984 - 02/1986; to Jersey European Airways as G-OJSY 03/1986; to Connectair 05/1988 - 10/1988; to Business Air 10/1988 - 24/05/1995; to BAC Express 26/05/1995; to Associated Aviation as 5N-BBZ 10/2000.

G-RMSS   SH3604   29/12/1982

Registered G-RMSS by Short Brothers 30/12/1982; to Fairflight Charters Ltd 06/01/1983; to Air Ecosse 06/01/1983; to Short Brothers 25/04/1985 - 16/05/1985; to Loganair 08/1986 - 11/1986; **to Manx Airlines 02/1987**; to Guernsey Airlines 02/05/1987; transferred to Aurigny Air Services 03/09/1987; to Connectair, renamed Air Europe Express 01/02/1989, as G-BPCO 02/1988; to Fairflight Charters Ltd 15/03/1991; to Gill Air 10/04/1991; re-registered G-OLAH 14/08/1991; to Air UK 13/03/1995 - 08/1995.

G-SALU   SH3628   02/12/1983

Delivered to Genair as G-BKZR 15/12/1983; repossessed by Short Brothers 11/09/1984; to Air Business as OY-MMC 23/10/1984; to Short Brothers as G-SALU 10/1985; to Loganair 10/01/1986 - 28/04/1986; **to Manx Airlines 02/1988 - 13/02/1989**; to Air Europe Express as G-0AEX 02/1989 - 15/03/1991; to Euroworld Airways, renamed Cityflyer Express 03/02/1992, as G-BKZR 23/08/1991; to Streamline Aviation 11/1992 - 03/1993; to Gill Air 26/06/1994 - 31/08/1994; to Shorts Brothers as N424SA 04/10/1994; Converted to C-23B Sherpa (c/n 3404) 12/1996; to United States Air Force as 94-0310 31/03/1997.

G-VBAC   SH3736   23/02/1983   Used on Belfast - Edinburgh wet leased from BAC Express.

Registered G-BOEJ by Short Brothers 03/1988; to Hazeton Airlines as VH-MJU 26/11/88; to Fairchild Aircraft Inc 14/07/1995; withdrawn from use and stored Sydney, Australia 07/1995; to BAC Express Airlines 08/1997; re-registered G-VBAC 15/09/1997; to Jersey European Airways 24/10/1997 - 04/1998.

G-WACK   SH3611   05/05/1983

Delivered to British Midland Airways as G-BMAJ 01/05/1983; **to Manx Airlines as G-WACK 28/04/1986 - 16/04/1987 and 07/1987 - 07/1988**; to Loganair 07/1988; **transferred to British Regional Airlines 27/01/1997**; to Loganair 01/01/1998; to Pacific Coastal Airlines as C-GPCE 16/03/1999

Snias/Aerospatiale ATR-72

Length	89'5", 27.25 m		**Wingspan**	88'9", 27.05 m
Height	25'1", 7.65 m		**Wing Area**	656 sq ft, 60.94 sq m
Cruising Speed	327 mph, 284 knots		**Seats**	74
Range	830 miles, 1334 km		**Maximum Altitude**	25,000', 7620 m
Engines	2 x Pratt & Whitney PW127 Turboprops			

Manx/BRAL Registration	*Construction Number*	*First flew*	
G-UKTJ	509	11/12/1997	

Registered F-WWLC by Aero International (Regional); to Air UK (renamed KLM UK 01/04/1999) as G-UKTJ 19/12/1997; to Gill Airways 31/10/1999 - 04/02/2000; **to British Regional Airlines 26/03/2000 - 09/2000**; to Vietnam Airlines as VN-B242 26/09/2000.

G-UKTK	519	13/01/1998	Stood in for G-UKTM on occasions.

Registered F-WWLQ by Avions de Transport Regional; to Air UK (renamed KLM UK 01/04/1999) as G-UKTK 30/01/1998; to Gill Airways 19/01/2000 - 11/02/2000.

G-UKTL	523	26/02/1998	Stood in for G-UKTM on occasions.

Registered F-WWLD by Avions de Transport Regional; to Air UK (renamed KLM UK 01/04/1999) as G-UKTL 03/1998; to Gill Airways 31/10/1999 - 11/02/2000; to Vietnam airlines as VN-B246 10/2000.

G-UKTM	508	16/12/1996	In service in British Airways World livery with Chatham Wing tail.

Registered F-WWLU by Aero International (Regional); to Air UK (renamed KLM UK 01/04/1999) as G-UKTM 23/04/1998; **to British Regional Airlines 31/10/1999.**

G-UKTN	496	29/09/1996	Stands in for G-UKTM on occasions.

Registered F-WWLT by Avions de Transport Regional; to Air UK (renamed KLM UK 01/04/1999) as G-UKTN 04/06/1998.

Vickers Viscount 806,813,816

Length	85'0" 25.91m		**Wingspan**	93'8" 28.55m
Height	26'9", 8.15 m		**Wing Area**	963 sq ft, 89.06 sq m
Cruising Speed	320 mph, 278 knots		**Seats**	73
Range	1587 miles, 2550 km		**Maximum Altitude**	27,000 ft, 8229.6 m
Engines	4x Rolls Royce dart 520, 530, 525			

Manx/BRAL Registration	*Construction Number*	*First flew*
G-AOYL	261	23/01/1958

Delivered to British European Airways as G-AOYL 14/02/1958; to BKS Air Transport, renamed Northeast Airlines 01/11/1970, 28/05/1968; merged to British Airways 01/04/1974; to British Air Ferries 27/01/1984; **to Manx Airlines 13/05/1986 - 22/05/1986**; broken up at Southend 02/1993

G-AOYM   262   26/02/1958

Delivered to British European Airways as G-AOYM 19/03/1958; to Cambrian Airways 08/11/1971; merged to British Airways 01/04/1974; to British Air Ferries 27/01/1984; **to Manx Airlines 21/02/1985 - 07/10/1985**; to Lineas Aereas Canarias as EC-DYC 25/10/1985; stored Canary Islands 05/1989.

G-AZNA   350   07/12/1958

Delivered to South African Airways as ZS-CDX 20/12/1958; re-registered ZS-SBX but not used; re-registered G-AZLU for British Midland Airways but not used; to British Midland Airways as G-AZNA 02/1972 **to Manx Airlines 11/1982 - 06/10/1984 and 10/1985 - 16/11/1985**; to BAe 07/05/1986; to British Midland Airways 07/05/1986; **to Manx Airlines 02/1988 - 02/1988**; to Baltic Airlines 01/08/1988; to Gambia Air Shuttle 02/1989 - 12/1989; to Hot Air 05/1990 - 09/1990; broken up Southend 01/1991.

G-BFZL   435   24/08/1959

Registered VH-TVR for Trans Australia Airlines but not used; converted to V836 04/1960; to Union Carbide & Carbon Corporation as N40N 17/05/1960; to Royal Australian Air Force as A6-435 08/1964; to Alda Corporation as N40NA 11/1969; to Jet Air Australia as VH-EQP 12/1969; to 501 Sultan of Oman's Air Force 06/1971; to Royal Swazi National Airways as 3D-ACM 12/09/1978 but not used; to British Midland Airways as G-BFZL 03/1979; **to Manx Airlines 02/10/1983 - 26/11/1983 and 16/11/1985 - 28/10/1988**; to BAe 11/1988; to Baltic Airlines 11/11/1988; **to Manx Airlines 11/04/1989 - 20/05/1990**; to British World Airlines 06/04/1993; to Heli Jet Aviation leased 04/1997; re-registered ZS-NNI 06/03/1998.

G-BLOA   259   09/12/1957

Delivered to British European Airways as G-AOYJ 08/01/1958; to Cyprus Airways 28/10/1965 - 05/1970; to Cambrian Airways 15/10/70; merged to British Airways 01/04/1974; to British Air Ferries 14/04/1981; to Air Algerie 09/05/1981 - 09/1981; to Panavia Air Cargo Ltd 04/01/1984; to British Air Ferries 04/01/1984; re-registered G-BLOA 02/08/1984; **to Manx Airlines 01/10/1984 - 21/02/1985 and 07/10/1985 - 10/1985**; to Guernsey Airlines 24/06/1986 - 09/1987; to Securicor Air 03/01/1989 - 01/1990; to British World Airlines 06/04/1993; broken up 08/1996.

The final Viscount operated by Manx was G-BFZL (c/n 435). An 816 series machine, it was powered by four Rolls Royce Dart 525 engines which produced a very distinctive noise. In October 1988 this aircraft had the dubious honour of being the last Viscount to operate a scheduled service out of London Heathrow. It is seen here getting airborne from Ronaldsway.

Manx Airlines